Modern Liberty

"A spirited, sophisticated manifesto . . . his achievement is to show both the reach of his libertarian ideals and, in a spirit of self-scrutiny, their necessary limits. . . . Fried's most valuable contribution is to highlight the abiding tension between personal liberty and the 'welfare administrative state.' . . . As Fried emphasizes, to his great credit, constitutional liberty in America is a matter not just of individual rights but of self-government too."
—Gary Rosen, *New York Times Book Review*

"A sharp examination of the idea of liberty in the modern, democratic state. . . . It's a tribute to the author's seriousness and good will that he makes a strong and vigorous case for both sides of each argument. . . . Even those predisposed to disagree will find it hard to counter his rigorous arguments. Liberty is fortunate to have such a reasoned and persuasive voice as its champion."
—*Kirkus Reviews*

"Charles Fried's *Modern Liberty* is a thoughtful, adventurous, and—for me at least—vexingly invigorating book. Why vexingly invigorating? Because on many of the controversial issues that Fried addresses, I strongly favor the opposite side to the one he espouses, and I found myself forced again and again to rise to the challenge of clarifying my own convictions."
—Stephen Greenblatt, best-selling author of *Will in the World*

"Charles Fried offers his readers an intellectual feast."
—Floyd Abrams

"Charles Fried's *Modern Liberty* offers a stunningly insightful and engaging narrative on such concepts as liberty, equality, beauty, respect, the state, and the rule of law. In a far-ranging and original analysis, Fried explains how these fundamental ideas interact and continue to have meaning in a constantly changing, ever more complex society."

—Geoffrey R. Stone, author of *Perilous Times*

"Charles Fried, in this book, led me to rethink the nature of liberty. . . . He means to be provocative and is, making us think about profound issues."   —Anthony Lewis

"In *Modern Liberty*, Charles Fried, who has distinguished himself as both public servant and professor, has written an insightful meditation on the fate of traditional concepts of liberty in the modern welfare state. He finds much to praise in the older virtues, and weaves a distinctive path that starts with the first principles of political philosophy and winds its way through modern disputes on education, speech, and much else. Readers are well advised to join him on his journey."   —Richard Epstein

"Fried, President Ronald Reagan's solicitor general, doesn't discount the worth of beauty, glory, equality, and other 'good' virtues, but he argues that they all pale beside the core American value of liberty."   —*Historywire.com*

"Fried delivers a strong discussion of contemporary liberty, sharing his ample knowledge of public policy and giving the reader a breathtakingly nuanced review of an often elusive concept."

—Paras D. Bhayani, *The Harvard Crimson*

"*Modern Liberty* remains accessible and readable while engaging with some deep, philosophical questions. It should be widely read."   —Clarissa Woodberry, *Culturewars.org.uk*

MODERN LIBERTY

AND THE LIMITS OF GOVERNMENT

Also by Charles Fried

An Anatomy of Value

Medical Experimentation: Personal Integrity and Social Policy

Right and Wrong

Contract as Promise

Order and Law: Arguing the Reagan Revolution

Making Tort Law (with David Rosenberg)

*Saying What the Law Is: The Constitution
in the Supreme Court*

Issues of Our Time

Ours has been called an information age, but, though information has never been more plentiful, ideas are what shape and reshape our world. "Issues of Our Time" is a series of books in which some of today's leading thinkers explore ideas that matter in the new millennium. The authors—beginning with the philosopher Kwame Anthony Appiah, the lawyer and legal scholar Alan Dershowitz, and the Nobel Prize–winning economist Amartya Sen—honor clarity without shying away from complexity; these books are both genuinely engaged and genuinely engaging. Each recognizes the importance not just of our values but also of the way we resolve the conflicts among those values. Law, justice, identity, morality, and freedom: concepts such as these are at once abstract and utterly close to home. Our understanding of them helps define who we are and who we hope to be; we are made by what we make of them. These are books, accordingly, that invite the reader to reexamine hand-me-down assumptions and to grapple with powerful trends. Whether you are moved to reason together with these authors, or to argue with them, they are sure to leave your views tested, if not changed. The perspectives of the authors in this series are diverse, the voices are distinctive, the issues are vital.

HENRY LOUIS GATES JR., SERIES EDITOR
W. E. B. DU BOIS PROFESSOR OF THE HUMANITIES
HARVARD UNIVERSITY

Issues of Our Time

Other titles

KWAME ANTHONY APPIAH
Cosmopolitanism: Ethics in a World of Strangers

AMARTYA SEN
Identity and Violence: The Illusion of Destiny

ALAN DERSHOWITZ
Preemption: A Knife That Cuts Both Ways

Forthcoming authors

WILLIAM JULIUS WILSON

LOUIS MENAND

CLAUDE STEELE

AMY GUTMANN

NICHOLAS LEMANN

ROLAND FRYER

MODERN LIBERTY

AND THE LIMITS OF GOVERNMENT

Charles Fried

W. W. NORTON & COMPANY
NEW YORK • LONDON

Interior art: Details from a fresco by Ambrogio Lorenzetti
(fl. c. 1311–1348). *Allegory of Good Government: Effects of Good Government in the City*, 1338–1339. Palazzo Pubblico, Siena, Italy.
Photograph credit: Scala / Art Resource, NY.

For information about permission to reproduce selections from this book,
write to Permissions, W. W. Norton & Company, Inc., New York, NY 10110

Manufacturing by Courier Westford

Library of Congress Cataloging-in-Publication Data

Fried, Charles, 1935–
Modern liberty : and the limits of government / Charles Fried. — 1st ed.
p. cm.
Includes bibliographical references and index.
ISBN-13: 978-0-393-06000-3 (hardcover)
ISBN-10: 0-393-06000-4 (hardcover)
1. Liberty. 2. State, The. I. Title.
JC585.F7575 2006
323.44—dc22

2006022060

ISBN 978-0-393-33045-1 pbk.

W. W. Norton & Company, Inc., 500 Fifth Avenue, New York, N.Y. 10110
www.wwnorton.com

W. W. Norton & Company Ltd., Castle House, 75/76 Wells Street,
London W1T 3QT

1 2 3 4 5 6 7 8 9 0

For my friends
Ronald Dworkin and Thomas Nagel
and in memory of
Robert Nozick and John Rawls
from whom I have learned so much

CONTENTS

PREFACE

Individual liberty in the welfare administrative state, the modern liberty of my title, has been on my mind at least since the 1960s. It is what I talked about with the four friends to whom I dedicate this book. Liberty has been implicated in one way or another in all my writing and teaching—on public and private law and on philosophy—and in my work in government. When Henry Louis Gates, Jr., the general editor of this series, asked me to contribute a volume on free speech, I declined, because I had just published a book on constitutional law, *Saying What the Law Is: The Constitution in the Supreme Court*, in which free speech is a principal topic. I proposed instead to broaden my horizon to liberty in general and to do it in a different way. My aspiration was to do for our time and liberal democratic societies what Friedrich Hayek did for his some sixty years ago in *The Road to Serfdom*, but without the apocalyptic thunder, with full acknowledgment of the good things that the post–New Deal world has done for almost everyone.

The challenge from the start has been to write a book that, while closely and fairly argued, at the same time is concrete, immediate, and personal, assuming no particular disciplinary background nor deploying any technical machinery—what my friend

Bruce Ackerman calls a book not for lawyers or academics but for human beings. In this I have been lucky in my editors: Roby Harrington, who kept that conception firmly before me, and Robert Weil, whose detailed, hectoring, appreciative, enthusiastic suggestions are rarely encountered in the publishing trade these days. Bruce Ackerman, Anthony Appiah, Stephen Breyer, Alan Dershowitz, Philip Fisher, Stephen Greenblatt, Janet Halley, Daryl Levinson, Richard Posner, Alan Stone, and William Stuntz have read drafts of all or part of the book at various stages and have given me much help and encouragement along the way. I thank them for their help, support, and friendship. I had valuable research and editorial help from my students Daniel Kelly, Tian Tian Mayimin, and especially Scott Dasovich.

—Charles Fried
Cambridge, Massachusetts
March 2006

CHAPTER 1

LIBERTY:
THE VERY IDEA

As a great popular leader [Mussolini] has said to an applauding multitude, "We will trample upon the decomposing body of the Goddess of Liberty."
    —W. B. Yeats, *Irish Independent*, August 4, 1924

He [l'abbé de Mably] hated individual liberty as one hates a personal enemy.   —Benjamin Constant

For Benjamin Constant—sometimes called the first apostle of modern liberty—"individual liberty is the first need of modern man."[1] He and his friend Madame de Staël, famous herself for her headstrong defense of liberty, survived the communitarian utopia of Robespierre's republic of terror only to be sent into exile by Napoleon's empire of the grandiose. "By liberty," he continues, "I mean the triumph—not just independence, the triumph—of individuality, as much over authority which would govern by despotism, as over the masses that would subordinate the minority to the majority." Constant returned to France to press for a British style constitutional monarchy, and when a grateful King Louis-Philippe paid off his many debts, Constant warned that this would not in the least prevent him from criticizing. It was said that he sold himself many times, but never delivered.[2] It is from Constant that Isaiah Berlin, in his celebrated *Two Concepts of Liberty*, took the contrast between the liberty of the ancients and the liberty of the moderns. Constant did not think them at all equivalent.[3] The liberty of the ancients, the liberty of a people to govern their own state subject to no other ruler, was often the best that men could hope for in a time when wealth was tied to land and the only escape was to exile, loneliness, and misery (think of Socrates choosing hemlock over exile from Athens), but Constant saw that this "liberty" often goes along with the total, Spartan annihilation of the individual. "It makes the individual a slave so that the people might be free."[4] In modern times a man can flee across borders with money in his wallet (or an "inverted Jenny" postage stamp worth a fortune, or an account number and a password) to build a new life elsewhere.[5] The liberty Constant valued was the liberty of a man to live his own life as he thought best. Then as now, America—to which Constant as a young man thought of emigrating[6]—is the closest thing to that ideal.

That is what I grew up to believe. My family and I were chased from Prague—that most prosperous, most commercial, most comfortable, bourgeois, and civilized of cities—by a homicidal maniac who, like Robespierre and Napoleon, had a vision of the glory of a nation and a people but cared nothing at all about persons. Then, with Hitler gone and my father on the point of taking us back to Czechoslovakia, that country was put in the pocket of another mass murderer with an even more lethal—because more plausible—nightmare vision, that of a universal equality, in which every man would belong to everyone and all men belong to the state.

It is of the liberty of persons, not peoples, it is of the liberty of the moderns, that (to borrow from the opening of the *Aeneid*) I sing.

The greatest enemy of liberty has always been some vision of the good. It might be the good of community engaged for the glory of a city, nation, race, or party. This is best captured in the image of tens of thousands of slaves broken by the labor of building the great Pyramids of Egypt, with a result that must have amazed, still amazes. True, as much as a reach for glory, these tombs may have been one of the more sensationally desperate attempts to overcome the fact of death, as sealed away with the preserved body of the pharaoh were the rich paraphernalia of his life. But then, glory has always been an avenue on the quest for immortality. The pharaohs may have built for their own glory and immortality, but always and everywhere many religions have been ready to sacrifice the liberty of those whose lives they touched—whether as adherents or not—to what they took to be the greater glory of their gods. Power, magnificence, and beauty are among the glories on which men have freely spent their own energies and the unwilling energies of others. But a way of life, whether of great simplic-

ity or of complex ritual observance, has also seemed a good so sur-
passing that others must be bent to its pursuit. Think of the rural
idyll-nightmare that Pol Pot sought to impose on Cambodia, or of
the complex observances of the medieval Japanese court.

Those who impose on others are often convinced that the
good they are after is a good as much for their victims as for themselves, and so they claim that there are no victims at all. But just
as often there is no thought of the good of the oppressed: Hitler
thought of the good and glory of the German race—supermen
ruled by a superman—a vision to which the elimination or subju-
gation of inferior races was integral, a vision in which those races
obviously were not asked to share. And indeed the question of
whose good it is—*cui bono*—in many instances misses the point
of this way of thinking, for it is the good in the abstract that is the
goal, not any particular person's good. The religious manifestation
is the clearest—the service of the gods is not the service of any
man. But running through this history of subjection and enslave-
ment is the claim of some to coerce the service of others, whether
for a common good, the good of the oppressor, or some good that
is an abstract from both and applicable to all.

In this catalogue of oppression, the idea of equality plays a
prominent yet ambiguous part. Liberty is so important that everyone should have as much of it as possible. But there is another
way of taking equality. Equality is so important that liberty, and
not only liberty but every other good thing, should be enjoyed only
to the extent that it may be enjoyed equally. In this second way,
equality is more like the other goods I have mentioned—national
glory or the service of the gods: it is a good that overrides the good
of particular persons insofar as the well-being of some are sacrificed to it, and even if the well-being of others is not enhanced.
This demands leveling down—deliberately hurting some people,
without helping others—if that is the only way to come closer to

equality. This was Pol Pot's project as he emptied the cities of Cambodia and killed or drove into the fields the educated and most prosperous townspeople: equality as a Great Pyramid. The Great Pyramid view of equality subordinates the goods—the well-being of individuals—to that one great abstraction.

We may know what counts as the power of a nation: its wealth or its successful conquests. Those who seek the glory of their gods seem to know what makes for that glory. But what is liberty? Here is a first, very general idea.

Liberty Is Individuality Made Normative

Individuals come first.[7] Whoever says otherwise is trading in metaphors. There are societies, nations, families, teams, but they are all made up of individual persons. Together persons create traditions, adhere to religions, make up communities, constitute the spirit of a time or place. Individuals inhabit traditions as they inhabit the societies and nations they constitute. They may be said to inhabit the language and culture to which they contribute and which contribute to their consciousness. But all these things—societies, nations, families, teams, traditions, religions, languages, and cultures—are the products of individual persons. There would be no language if no one had ever spoken it, although it can be written down and recorded and in that sense takes on a life of its own. So also a culture or a society (or corporation or football team) can be said to have a life of its own. Individuals move through these entities, and when they are gone the entities are still there—though changed in large or imperceptible degrees by the persons who have moved through them. But the individual is primary in the sense that only individuals have eyes, ears, mouths, hands, and brains, and it is only by individuals making, saying, drawing, writing and other individuals seeing, hearing, and understanding that languages are spoken and remembered, that traditions are felt and passed on.

Everything that matters to a person or to persons in general, everything humanly of value, is first of all experienced by individual persons. I now take the next step; and it is a large one. Everything that matters to persons, that is humanly significant, is chosen by individual persons, is the responsibility of individual persons, one by one. Here, as I use the word *responsibility*, it is I who may be accused of dealing in metaphors, but consider the sense in which a belief—a quite ordinary belief—can be said to be chosen by the one who believes it. The matter of belief, whether it is what a person directly perceives of the outside world or what others tell him, must somehow come to a man's consciousness, and there he must weigh it, decide whether to credit it or to dismiss it as an illusion, a mistake, a falsehood. Overwhelmingly, these judgments are snap: almost everything I see I accept as really there without giving it a second thought, but I do give it a first thought. Mostly if someone tells me a simple thing like "Take your umbrella, it is raining," I do not pause to consider whether to accept that it is in fact raining. And yet I must take in what was said and make a snap judgment that the person who is talking to me is in earnest or joking, a normal observer or a madman. I may judge credulously, impetuously, foolishly, or ignorantly, but these are all modes of belief and they are mine.

And so it is with my judgments of what I should do, what is good or bad, right or wrong. However much my choices may be influenced by prejudice, emotion, fear of others, it is still I who must choose before I act.[8] And the beliefs, choices, and actions that make up the human world are those of individuals—discrete points of perception, thought, judgment, and choice. They may coalesce in cultures, spirits of the time, but these are made up of individual perceptions, conclusions, choices, actions. And each individual experiences these as ineluctably his, whatever else they may be. In this sense he is responsible for all of them.

In addition to judgments and choices, so the pains and pleasures, the satisfactions and disappointments, the passions that give my life energy, are ineluctably mine. This has nothing to do with selfishness or altruism. Whether I take pleasure only in comfort and luxury or my happiness consists in the beauties of art and nature or in the thriving of my family, friends, or all humanity, still it is I who seek these goods and am elated or dejected by attaining them or failing to attain them. Again, this is not at all to say that I choose the good of humanity or the production of great beauty because of the satisfaction it procures for me; I feel the satisfaction (or dejection) because these things are good in themselves. If by some magic I had to choose between the satisfaction and the thing itself, I would choose the thing itself.[9] So the lover seeks the good of his beloved, not because of the pleasure he attains when the beloved is well but for her sake. (Think of Rick on the runway in *Casablanca* as Ilsa and Laszlo make their escape.) And still all of these goods—high and low, selfish and generous—are sought by us because of what we judge them to be. They are *our* goods.

Finally, this individualism should not be confused with solipsism. What I have been arguing does not at all commit me to the proposition that whatever an individual chooses or experiences as his good is therefore good after all. There may be—I believe there is—a fact of the matter about what is good or bad, right or wrong, worthwhile or degraded. The choosing individual may be profoundly mistaken, superficial, criminal, shallowly selfish; that he chooses as he does, does not determine the judgment on what he does. He is responsible for his beliefs, judgments, choices, and actions. To argue that because they are his, they cannot be good or bad in themselves is just a mistake; it is a mistake that deprives a man of responsibility.

It is this rock-bottom, indigestible fact of each person's lonely individuality, his ultimate responsibility for his own beliefs, judgments, and choices, that grounds our demand that we be free, that is the ground for our liberty. When others try to force me to do what I judge I do not want to do, or try to trick me into believing what I would not otherwise believe, they attack my person at its deepest level. Because that is where the attack on our liberty comes, it follows that there is a difference between what others do to me and what they merely allow to happen to me when they will not help me or get out of my way. In doing to me, they do indeed take my person into account and make that part of their project. In refusing to help or get out of my way, they may fail to acknowledge me as a judging, feeling, choosing individual, but in doing something *to* me they acknowledge that fact and use it for their own purposes. They (try to) deprive me of my liberty.

Liberty is individuality made normative. The person who disregards me—turns away or runs over me—ignores my individuality; he pays no mind to the fact that I have a distinct consciousness, distinct plans, distinct judgments. For example, the man who throws me out of a window onto his enemy in the street below in a sense uses me—but as an object, a dead weight, not as a thinking, responsible being. It is the man who takes account of my individuality—my thinking, reasoning, judgment—and forces me to bend my will to his who violates my liberty. His plan depends on the fact that I have plans, and he makes me make his plans part of my plans. I am the means to his ends— that is, I as an independent, responsible consciousness. A violation of liberty tears something: a man recognizes me, recognizes me as being a person like him, but then contradicts that recognition by using against me and for himself the very things that make him and me persons. It is this relationship between us that implicates liberty.

Now you may be thinking that as a thinking, feeling being, I have plans of my own—selfish or generous—and these plans (what might be called for short my good, or my goods) are what I care about. And these plans may be frustrated as much by someone who runs over me or passes me by as by someone who uses me. More, there is scarcely anything I can accomplish without others: I would not have been conceived or born, reached maturity, learned language without others. If I had been ignored, I would have died. The success of my plans always depends on others. Yes, but as we acknowledge that, notice how it is that we depend on each other. We depend on each other to deal with us— for us and against us—as thinking, choosing beings: as persons, as individuals (perhaps not in our conception and infancy, but soon after that). So all these good things implicate liberty, because they depend on our eliciting, discouraging, modifying other people's choices; they implicate how we treat each other as persons and not as inert objects to be ignored or obstacles to be got out of the way. The running over and passing by are secondary to our dealings with each other as persons. We run over or pass by each other on our way to something else, in pursuit of some plan, and *that* plan almost always depends on cooperating with or using others—their capacities to understand, value, and choose.

Liberty is implicated when we take those capacities into account. Consider two opposite ways in which we take into account other persons and their distinct capacities as individuals: we can cooperate with them or we can coerce them. (I use the term *coercion* to cover threats or orders, not physical restraint—it

is the difference between pointing a gun at a prisoner while order-
ing him to move and frog-marching him.) In cooperation we elicit
choices by inviting the other to join in our choices, to make our
choices his. Cooperation can be made to look like coercion—the
offer you cannot refuse.[10] Take an extreme and obvious example:
the bank manager can be said to cooperate with the bank robber
by opening the vault to save a hostage's life. And a less obvious
example: the landlord insists on a greatly increased rent when
renewing the lease of a successful restaurant that has over the
years come to be identified with a particular neighborhood. At the
other extreme, consider Mozart and the librettist da Ponte working together to create *The Marriage of Figaro,* or the joining of
lovers. In all of these examples—even the bank robbery—individuals make use of each other as persons; in all, liberty is implicated;
but only in the first example, that of the bank manager, is it clear
that liberty is *violated.* It will be my job in succeeding chapters to
unravel when liberty is violated and when it is invoked. (We will
see that a complete idea of liberty implies a notion of rights, and
others can trespass on my rights inadvertently, heedlessly, as well
as willfully and viciously. I may, and the state should, protect my
rights in both cases. But the trespasser conceives of me differently
in the two cases, and the extent and kind of justified defense of
my rights will differ too.)

In the rest of *Modern Liberty* I will try to make this abstract
notion—liberty as individuality made normative, the soul of modern liberty—more concrete, to show why and how it matters, not
in easy contrast to pharaohs or Pol Pot or even contemporary
China or Iran or Cuba, but in modern, prosperous, democratic
societies. So instead of bogeymen drawn from history's chamber
of horrors, I will put before you and keep coming back to three

examples drawn from places that in many ways are model decent and liberal democracies. I choose examples of impositions that are neither brutal, extreme, nor all-encompassing, but for all that they still get under our skin, because they seem to offend against liberty—not democratic liberty but what Constant called the liberty of the moderns.

Three Gentle Challenges

The language police.

In 1977 the French-speaking majority of the province of Quebec enacted the Quebec Charter of the French Language to assure, after what they felt had been two centuries of domination and humiliation by the English-speaking minority, that French Canadian culture and the French language would remain the culture and language of the province.[11]

The charter had a deep effect on the feel of life in Quebec. Here are some ways in which government officials applied the charter. The Montreal Chinese Hospital caters to elderly Chinese patients, most of whom speak only Chinese. But the Office of the French Language ("the language police") would not allow the hospital to advertise for Chinese-speakers to fill two of three vacant nursing positions. An English-speaking Ukrainian father who had been sent to a French immersion school as a boy in Winnipeg was denied the right to send his seven-year-old son to an English-language school when he and his English-speaking wife moved to Quebec, because he was classified as a French-speaking parent. They decided to home-school the boy. A grandmother was unable to place a catalogue order for a talking doll to be shipped to her six-year-old grandchild, who lived in a town across the river in

Quebec Province, because the doll spoke only English. A Montreal Jewish stonemason was threatened with prosecution
because his sign, made by his grandfather fifty years before, had
Hebrew characters (five of them) that were larger than the French
characters for "gravestone maker." And the owner of an English-
language paper was ordered to hand over photographs taken of an
inspector from the "language police" who was herself photographing as part of an inspection to check whether French was as
prominent as English in the signs posted in the newsroom.[12] The
newspaper was accused of hindering the official in her work. (The
first two of these bureaucratic impositions were eventually repu-
diated by courts or higher authorities.)[13]

In New York and London, English-speaking people expect that
they will be served in English in stores, that their children will be
taught in English, that when they go to court for a speeding ticket,
the judge will address them in English. More and more businesses, hospitals, and public institutions in the United States
post signs in English and Spanish or offer Spanish in their communications. And translators and interpreters into many languages are available to witnesses and parties, or even required to
be present, in court proceedings. But still, in the United States,
the United Kingdom, and Australia, no one would doubt that he
is in an English-speaking world. The same would be true for
French in France, German in Germany, Japanese in Japan. The
frequent accommodations I mention above ("If you wish to continue in Spanish, press 1") hardly challenge that. In spite of
them—maybe even because of them—an English-speaker is at
home in the United States, while the person who presses 1 feels
just that: accommodated, which of course is very nice. Quebecers
will tell you that they just want the same thing that Americans,
Britons, the French, and the Japanese have: to feel at home in
their own country.[14]

Health care for all.

This example comes from Quebec too. It is a refinement on a scheme, Health Canada, that obtains throughout the country and that Canadians are very proud of. To care for the sick has always been a duty of charity and now is generally understood as an obligation of a decent society. But in a complicated, modern state, meeting this obligation demands complicated systems. Doctors, hospitals, and medicines are ever more expensive as they seem ever more able to hold off the sickness and death that terrify us all. To some it seems that these systems must be total; everyone must be included. The rich or the health-obsessed should not be allowed to escape to expensive private sanatoriums, and greedy doctors should not be allowed to cater to them there. Too many skilled doctors and nurses might move to the luxury end of the system. This would take away from the care available at the lower end, and give the lie to the notion that being cared for in sickness and pain is a common entitlement of citizenship. Inevitably some people would have to suffer longer before relief came, the relief might not be as good, and some might even die.

In Canada the government pays for all medical care. The quality of care is good, but waiting lists are often very long—with grave or even lethal consequences. Canadians can buy medical services outside the system, but in Quebec there is a flat prohibition against buying or selling private health insurance for services that can be obtained from the public health system. And providers—doctors and hospitals—may not work both inside and outside the system. This has the predictable and intended result of making the one government-provided system inescapable except for those rich enough to travel outside the province, and even then they may not buy insurance to cover the expense of the expedition. (In 2005 the Supreme Court of Canada held in a four-to-three decision that limiting citizens to the state system with its sometimes life-threatening delays violated constitutional rights to life and personal security. Some hope that with a change in the makeup of the court, the decision may shift to the position of the dissenters: that the ban is justified to protect the one-tier system and equality of access. In fact things seem to be moving in the opposite direction, with private, technically illegal surgery centers springing up all over Canada.)[15]

Other countries, like the United Kingdom, provide universal government-funded health care but allow doctors and clinics to offer health care on a private basis, and there exists a thriving business in insurance that offers to cover the cost of such private care. All public systems in effect ration the care they give by a combination of bureaucratic allocation, quality limitation, and queuing. The private alternatives, where they are allowed, allocate and ration too, but through the prices they charge patients and the fees earned by providers.

Wal-Mart in Vermont.

Wal-Mart, the largest of the "big box" retailers, prospers by opening enormous stores, often more than 150,000 square feet in size (something like three football fields), in suburban locations and offering a very wide range of goods at low prices. Some state and local governments have used zoning and other laws to make it harder for stores like Wal-Mart to open, and the National Trust for Historic Preservation has gone so far as to put the whole state of Vermont on its 2004 list of most endangered historic places in order to support defensive legal measures there. This is what the trust had to say:

> With historic villages and downtowns, working farms, winding back roads, forest-wrapped lakes, spectacular mountain vistas

and a strong sense of community, Vermont has a special magic that led *National Geographic Traveler* magazine to name the state one of "the World's Greatest Destinations." Yet in recent years, this small slice of America has come under tremendous pressure from the onslaught of big-box retail development. . . .

The likely result: degradation of the Green Mountain State's unique sense of place, economic disinvestment in historic downtowns, loss of locally-owned businesses, and an erosion of the sense of community that seems an inevitable by-product of big-box sprawl.[16]

Obviously a store as large as a Wal-Mart eats up a lot of space, especially if you add the parking area and the other large retailers that often come in next to it. But given the size of the state and the relatively sparse population, there is a great deal of farmland and forest left. The real mechanism of the "degradation" of which the trust speaks is economic. The retailers long located along the main streets of nearby small cities and towns cannot compete with Wal-Mart either in price or in variety of goods. With better roads, the spread of housing beyond the former peripheries of suburban and rural cities and towns, and the increase of two- and three-car households, Main Street retailers have been losing their customers, leaving abandoned and lifeless the centers of towns and small cities, with their picturesque main streets, their general stores, family pharmacies, and soda fountains, where townspeople used to congregate to shop and enjoy the opportunity of meeting friends and neighbors. These chance encounters weave a web of familiarity and mutual concern that helps to create and maintain a sense of civic responsibility. Parking lots, superstore shopping aisles, and checkout lines are unlikely to come to life as such informal civic forums. Rather, they will speed the tendency toward a more atomized, private citizenry.

But economic pressures squeeze out local shopowners and their Main Street sites only because the people who used to shop on Main Street prefer the big-box plazas and the lower prices. After all, Main Street grew up in an earlier time not to provide an agoralike experience to townspeople but because the townspeople found it convenient to be able to go to a concentrated area and walk from the place where they bought groceries to the hardware store and on to the town hall to carry out their business. The quality and variety was greater than what the peddlers traveling from door to door could offer, and much of what people wanted was immediately available, so they would not have to wait until the mail took their order to the catalogue store and weeks later delivered the goods. The Wal-Marts offer a greatly magnified version of the same advantages. For reasons beyond the power of Vermont legislators to control, there is an incomparably greater variety of goods available to ordinary citizens at prices many can afford. So Main Street will be abandoned for the superstore shopping mall, only because that is where people can get what they want. If the townspeople did not shop at Wal-Mart but stubbornly patronized the family dry goods store, Main Street would prosper and Wal-Mart would fail.[17]

Why Are These Stories About Liberty?

In times past (and still in some parts of the world) people have had little or no voice in the choice of those who would govern them. They have been (and are) imprisoned, beaten, and killed because of what they say or print, or because of their religious or political beliefs, or because they may compete with more favored persons, or for no discernible reason at all. They have been forbidden from marrying or even meeting certain people. They have been made to wear certain clothing. They have been excluded from certain work or kept at particular kinds of work. They have been made to stay in the city, region, or country where they lived, or kept out of certain towns and regions, or removed from the towns and regions where they lived. Perhaps we might learn what liberty is and why we value it by looking at these gross violations, but our unanalyzed intuitions about them are too uniform, the good reasons for rejecting these impositions too many and strong.

That is why you will find nowhere in this book about liberty a discussion of many of the issues that occupy those who are called, with perfect justice, civil libertarians: the power to arrest, to search for papers, and to wiretap. There is no discussion of jury trial or preventive detention or the death penalty. These are without doubt important features in the landscape, whether it is a landscape of liberty or of tyranny and terror. But they are never done for their own sake, except by madmen. They are always things done for the sake of advancing or protecting some order or other, some conception of the good society. The most liberal of societies must have police, prosecutors, and prisons to protect individual liberties against internal predators and armies to protect against external aggressors. My attention here is drawn to the good of liberty itself as the purpose of society, and much less to the question of what practical measures may or must be allowed to protect that liberty. If you are thinking that there is a connection between the two, that a society which values individuals accepts restraints even in dealing with people accused of preying on others and breaking those restraints, I agree with you. But I leave that to other books and other days. Instead of considering such matters, which we have such clear intuitions about that they clarify little of what liberty is or why we care about it, I begin with subtler, more plausible impositions, to ask whether they are dep-

rivations of liberty at all. In looking at the justifications offered for
these impositions we can begin to understand what modern liberty is, why we value it, and what its limits are.

All these impositions share the characteristic that they are chosen by democratic states in which those who are imposed on have
full political participation. Right away we see—as Constant
saw—that democratic participation is not a straightforward guar-
antor of liberty. Compare my examples with measures that impose
taxes and spend the revenue on the usual range of governmental
functions. At both the taxing and the spending ends of that
process, there are always people who would do it otherwise, but
only the most extreme among them claim that these forced contributions deprive them of their liberty. Nor do many who object
to their government's foreign policy or even its decisions to go to
war claim that they have been unjustly deprived of their liberty.
Between taxes and war is a whole range of governmental action,
from regulations of the sale of alcohol to zoning ordinances, that
people may not like but go along with, grumbling the while. Why
is it that hackles go up—if they do—in the examples I have given?

Here is a first attempt at an answer. In each of these challenges, there is what I would call a sense of personal *enlistment*
into a cause one does not share. I use the word *enlistment* to suggest that that may be a closer involvement than in, say, the cases
in which a government uses the tax revenues a dissenter has contributed for purposes that the dissenter objects to. But of course
enlistment is just what happens in the most literal way to the
unwilling recruit into the military in wartime. The Quebec Charter of the French Language, for example, enlists the person who
would rather speak English to his customers or put up a sign in
Chinese or Hebrew only in the sense that he must either use
French or be silent altogether. The doctors and patients in the
exclusive state health-care system also can choose to forgo treat-

ing or being treated, or Canadian patients can come to the United States, just as Vermont shoppers can travel to neighboring states to make their purchases or shop by mail or on-line. Indeed, the exit option may be thought to draw the teeth of any but the most draconian impositions.[18]

Who Imposes on Whom?

In all three examples, those who resent and would resist these schemes do not think of themselves as wanting to harm other people, or even as taking anything away from them. Compare taxes and military service. The evader palpably withdraws a contribution to the provision of a good that he continues to enjoy and everyone else pays for. And even if he claims not to enjoy it, it is difficult for him to forgo the benefit. In my three cases, by contrast, it would seem that there is no such unfair benefiting. People who want to speak French and conduct their dealings among one another in French can continue to do that even though some signs have large Hebrew letters. Doctors are not prevented from treating and patients from being treated within the government system just because some choose to operate in a parallel system. And so too those who like shopping in a quaint old Vermont town center are free to do so, even though their neighbors prefer the vulgar advantages of greater choice and lower prices in the big-box store at the edge of town. The Chinese-, Hebrew-, or English-speaker, the well-healed patient, or the bargain-minded shopper believes that he is not interfering with those who subscribe to the virtues of the French language, of generous, free health care, or of the charms of old-time village shopping. He resents being recruited into a cause he does not believe in, when his participa-

tion is required only because the schemes might be abandoned if
alternatives were seen to exist. This does seem to be a different
mechanism from that which may undermine a regime of military
service or tax contributions if free riders were seen to enjoy their
benefits without sharing their burdens.

In the medical and Wal-Mart examples, the complaint may be
narrowed to the unnecessary forced participation in a project that
the complainers might be willing to support with their tax dollars.
The sense is that in this way their liberty to do as they wish has
been interfered with, not simply to allow their fellows to arrange
their lives and communities as they wish but also to seal off alternatives to dissenters just so these alternatives are driven from the
scene altogether. It is as if the majority not only wanted to be able
to arrange their community but did not want others to live differently, even if that did not interfere with the community's preferred
arrangement. It is the cramming of a way of life down people's
throats that seems the offense. And it is an offense committed in
the most benign and democratic of places.

The prevailing majorities in Quebec and Vermont would very
likely object to this characterization. In each instance they would
claim that they would gladly respect the dissenters' rights to
speak, to seek and give medical care, to shop where they wish, if
only their choices did not keep the majority from choosing the
alternative arrangements they prefer. The majorities claim that the
Quebec French language would die out if others were not
recruited to it, that the health-care system would unravel if alternatives were allowed, that choice would ruin Vermont towns. In
all three cases, the "free" behavior of the dissenters is "free" only
in a sense internal to the dissenting group—their behavior does
harm others outside the group (it imposes what economists call
negative externalities) by preventing the majority from accom-
plishing what they choose to accomplish. How does it do that?

If a critical mass of inhabitants do not speak French in their regular dealings, the French-speaking atmosphere of Quebec would be eroded and soon the pressure from the surrounding English-speaking world would become irresistible, even though a majority want to resist it. What the majority is trying to do is create an atmosphere like the one that exists in most of France (or, in respect to English, in most parts of the United States), where the use of French is the tacit norm, a norm that needs no enforcement because it is so generally observed that deviations do not threaten to undermine it—indeed, it will survive even if those who adhere to it are cheerfully ready to depart from it for those who may need to be accommodated. In a sense it is not normative at all, because there are no sanctions—not even a momentary frown—for departures from it, and that is because it is so generally observed. We say the people speak English (or French) *as a rule*, not because there is any rule requiring it but because that is just what generally happens. It is that happy and easy state of affairs that the majority wants to attain and maintain for the French language in Quebec. And they may well be right that without the elaborate rules of the Charter of the French Language, that chance would slip away and Montreal would become another polyglot Gotham in which the ambitious and the hip all speak English.

In much the same way, unless a practice, a norm, of equal treatment is established, then a system of universal free health care will melt away. Perhaps at first support for the public norm will be so high that people would be embarrassed to jump the queue; they are proud that in the adjoining hospital bed is the kindly woman from the checkout counter at the supermarket, who has just had the same treatment at the expert hands of the same surgeon, glad that they do not have to turn away in embarrassment from the cardiac wheezing of the woman at the cashier's desk who cannot afford the heart surgery that would make her breathe easy. But unless the norm is enforced, will not some and then more and more look for advantages in time or skill? What parent with a child suffering from serious illness would not look for the very best and promptest treatment? And if some will pay, others will take the pay, so that soon there will be two parallel systems of hospitals and clinics. After that it may be that although everybody pays for a system only some must rely on, the support for it among those who look to the speedier, more comfortable, perhaps better system will drop off; though in a minority, they will come to resent paying for what they do not use and will treat their taxes as an imposition or an act of charity. They will see less and less reason to insist vigilantly that the care be excellent, and because they are likely to be better informed and critical, their vigilance will be missed. The gap between the two systems will widen. That is the path the Canadians do not want to start down.

Finally, as to Wal-Martization, let us grant that almost all Vermonters would rather not see their quaint town centers boarded up and dilapidated. Many might even be willing to sacrifice the convenience and savings the big-box stores offer for the sake of keeping the country store, the soda fountain, and the family drugstore open. But how tempting it is to enjoy stopping by for a chat in front of the courthouse or bank but sneaking off to Wal-Mart when it comes to doing the Christmas shopping. (How many people from big cities and university towns celebrate the virtues of the few remaining idiosyncratic, independent bookstores, yet when the yen for a book strikes them at their desk or in the evening, go on-line and order it from Amazon.com and so drive another small nail into the coffin of the independent bookstore?)[19] This is a familiar phenomenon. A practice or a state of affairs depends on the cooperation of a large number of people, the defection of any one person is unnoticeable, and so the temptation to enjoy the benefits of the practice without making even the very small contribution called for is great. Unfortunately, since everyone is similarly situated and similarly tempted, the practice will unravel quite fast, and that is why some kind of enforcement mechanism is needed—a sanction larger than the small benefit gained from cheating, or, in the Wal-Mart example, closing off the alternative altogether.

In this sense, in a regime without coercion, the minority might be seen as imposing a veto on the majority. Imagine that two towns want to build a bridge across a river and so make travel between them easier. A few people do not want that. They think the bridge will spoil the view and increase traffic on the roads of both towns, and they do not much like the people in the neighboring town and do not want to see more of them in their streets and shops. There is no way that both the minority and the majority can have their way. Making the bridge a toll bridge will not solve the conflict. You cannot have a bridge, traffic, and visitors that only those who want them will be aware of.

So why are not the Charter of the French Language, Health Canada, and Vermont's anti–Wal-Mart regulation like that? Similarly, if a majority of citizens want roads, a police force, a national defense, and public parks, there is no easy way to limit the advantages these offer only to those who are willing to pay for them with their taxes. Even if we could exclude dissenters from some of these amenities (we might require a license to drive on the roads or even to be a passenger in a vehicle that does, or the fire brigade might fail to respond to calls from nonpayers), it is a characteristic of these goods that they procure indirect benefits (increased commerce, availability of goods, ease of access by visitors) from which nonpayers cannot be excluded. National defense is the paradigm, but the same is true of the general atmosphere of security that comes from a functioning police force. Indeed, if criminals could prey on nonpayers with impunity, even payers would be hurt, because the increase in the number of criminals would inevitably erode the security of the payers. The benefit enjoyed by nonpayers is an example of what is called a positive externality conferred by payers on nonpayers; the erosion of security for payers is a negative externality imposed by nonpayers on payers. And there is the problem that anyone can claim not to want the goods, thus avoiding paying his share for a good he in fact does want and would be willing to pay for. This would lead to a downward spiral, so that the majority could no longer get what it is ready to pay for, just as the citizens of Quebec or Vermont would be frustrated by a regime of free adherence—talk French if you want to, don't if you don't.

This is a serious objection. But I have chosen my three examples because there seem to be differences between them and the traditional public goods cases. It may well be that both the traditional public goods cases—roads, police protection, national defense—and my three examples involve negative and positive externalities, but the mechanisms by which those external benefits are captured and external harms are avoided are different. In my three cases the dissenters are not being asked to contribute— money is not the point, for we can imagine compelled labor to build roads, or a military draft—but rather are being asked to refrain from doing something they want to do. In fact the dissenters may be quite ready to contribute. The dissenting Quebecers may be quite ready *also* to speak French. The dissenting Vermonters may be ready to pay a subsidy to downtown merchants (a tax exemption for downtown businesses). And the dissenting Canadians may be ready to pay for a health-care system they do not use, just as parents who send their children to private schools still pay taxes to support public schools. So it is not the compelled contribution. It is compelling contribution by shutting off escape.

You might say that the taxes for the health-care system compel one to use it; the subsidy to the downtown merchants drives up Wal-Mart's prices, decreasing the advantage it enjoys. But the regulations I have been discussing do not just make alternatives less attractive (more costly); they close them off altogether. The only escape is by moving out of Quebec, going abroad for medical treatment, shopping in New Hampshire. One response to this resort to the exits has been to lock them (think of the Berlin Wall). And what is wrong with locking the exits, if departure will do the same kind of harm to these democratically chosen and perfectly reasonable goals that would be done by nonparticipation? Oh, but locking the exits goes too far; it is an offense to liberty. Yes, but how far is too far, if the regulation the refugee seeks to flee is not itself an improper restriction of liberty?

These benign, everyday examples pose the questions this book will try to answer. What is liberty, and how is it possible in modern society? How can one person's liberty square with the liberty of others? What are the goals for which it may seem it is worth sacrificing liberty? Constant celebrated the "triumph of individuality over the masses that would subordinate the minority to the majority." But is it not even more tyrannical to let the few frustrate the goals of the many?

In the next chapter I paint a picture—as sympathetic as I can make it—of ideals that compete with liberty to dominate and organize our individual and communal lives. I begin with beauty, but I mean it to be a stand-in for a whole group of ideals: the glory and power of a nation, of a race, or of a leader, the abstract ideal of community as something over and above the happiness and well-being of the individuals who make up that community. But of all the ideals that compete with liberty, none is as powerful or as attractive as equality. It shares with liberty the characteristic that it blankets the pursuit of all substantive goals, saying how they should be pursued. Both are adverbial notions: we pursue our goals freely or equally. Being free without being free to do *something* is an incomplete notion. So too perhaps we should all be equal; but equal in respect to what?

CHAPTER 2

LIBERTY AND ITS COMPETITORS

Since her separate peace with the Sultan and consequent estrangement from Spain and the Empire, Venice's relations with France had become of prime importance; and the Venetians, never reluctant to put on a show, had decided to give Henry a reception that he would long remember. At Marghera on the mainland the King was greeted by sixty senators in crimson velvet; thence he was conducted in a fleet of gilded gondolas to Murano, where a guard of honour of sixty halberdiers awaited him, in specially designed uniforms featuring the national colours of France, together with forty young scions of the leading Venetian families, who were to form his personal suite for the duration of his visit. His state entry to the city was planned for the next day; that same evening, however, he managed to slip out in a black cloak, unobserved, for a silent, secret journey through the canals.

—John Julius Norwich, *A History of Venice*

Beauty

Travelers, diplomats, and emperors coming to Venice report their astonishment not only at its wealth and magnificence but particularly at its beauty. State visitors might alight at the Piazzetta, between the high columns of St. George and the lion of St. Mark, be led between the Palace of the Doges and the three-hundred-foot Campanile to the vast Piazza of St. Mark, described by an earlier French visitor as the finest in the world. John Julius Norwich describes how, in 1574, when King Henry made his official entry into the city in the gold-encrusted state barge, the palaces along the Grand Canal were hung with cloth of gold and silk embroidered with his heraldic device, and throughout his visit there were banquets, parades, and performances. He posed for Tintoretto and called on the ninety-seven-year-old Titian, and, having been presented by the Signoria with an array of miniatures from which to take his pick, was granted an interlude with Veronica Franco, Venice's most celebrated courtesan. Norwich also tells that the Venetians had another point to make: one morning he visited the Arsenal to see the keel of a ship being laid, and that evening he saw the same ship launched—rigged, armed, and ready for war.

The reception for King Henry was a prelude and setting for high politics. A private visitor of no power but infinite discernment writing from his hotel balcony some three hundred years later—when Venice long had had no power—put it this way: *"Mes rêves sont devenus mon addresse."* ("My dreams have become my address.")[1]

For imperial Venice, beauty was an instrument of power, but the Venetians, like the Spartans and the Huns, might have relied on a reputation for strength and ferocity to terrorize those whom they wished to dominate. Here is what Gibbon says of Attila: "The haughty step and demeanor of the king of the Huns expressed the consciousness of his superiority above the rest of mankind; and he had a custom of fiercely rolling his eyes, as if he wished to enjoy the terror which he inspired."[2] Just as the Venetians impressed Henry on his visit, so Attila impressed the Roman ambassadors who went to meet him at the site of the Danubian city of Naissus: "The Huns left the riverbanks there heaped with human bones, and the stench of death was so great that no one could enter the city. Naissus was so devastated that Roman ambassadors passing through to meet with Attila several years later had to camp outside."[3] Beauty is just one of the ways in which to convey power, to assert mastery, to put others in awe.

Because it does put in awe, it is often hard to separate the awe from the beauty. Is a lavish display of rare gems truly beautiful, or does it put in awe because of its rarity and the wealth it shows? (In medieval and early Renaissance paintings, the gold was real gold and the blue, powdered lapis lazuli.) Does the Great Pyramid of Giza—until the nineteenth century the highest human structure—attain beauty after all because it is a created mountain, and mountains are truly beautiful? (Remember Thomas Carlyle: "What could be so vile as a pyramid two feet high?") And closer than the tie between beauty and power, wealth, or sheer enormity is the tie of beauty to sex.[4] Whatever the sexual attraction of a beautiful woman—and who knows what it is—it is impossible to untangle the sex from the beauty. Yet we experience a distinct gasp, a distinct awe for what is beautiful—though it is neither rich, rare, threatening, enormous, nor erotic: some music, some painting, poetry, a beautiful child. Like only a few other things, beauty is something we want for its own sake. Is liberty like that?

Liberty at first seems very different from beauty; it seems to be essentially facilitative. We are free—at liberty—to do this or that, to find this or that good, but beauty, while it may be facilitative—an instrument of power, for instance—is essentially valuable for its own sake. Where beauty is facilitative, as in the case of the Venetian pageant mounted for Henry III, it succeeds because those to whom it is directed as a device or inducement value it for its own sake. Yet liberty is spoken of with greater respect than, say, wealth, which is the very type of an instrumental good—it is worth only what it will buy. That is not to say that people will not trade liberty for other things, including wealth. There seems to be a paradox. Liberty is liberty to do as we choose, or at least to be free from restraints imposed by others on what we do. So why are not the things we choose rather than the liberty to pursue them of intrinsic worth?

In a small and beautiful book, *On Beauty and Being Just*, Elaine Scarry argues that there is an essential connection between beauty and justice. Her examples tend to the miniature: a petal, a moth the size of a child's thumbnail. Beauty is a form of symmetry, and symmetry connects to equality and justice, just as it does to truth, as when we speak of a beautiful proof in mathematics. Beauty takes us out of ourselves and in that modesty enables us to value not only other things but other persons. All this may be true. There is a connection between beauty and truth, beauty and symmetry and fairness, but it is not a necessary relationship. Beauty has been pursued with great disregard for the human cost in its production. It has celebrated waste and even exquisite cruelty. I think of Flaubert's *Salammbô*. Indeed, I would be more inclined to reverse Scarry's argument: justice and equality may sometimes themselves be beautiful; that is, they can delight beyond even our approbation of their moral correctness. Scarry's example is the perfect rhythm and unity in which the 170 free men in the triremes of the Periclean navy swept, "according to the pace of the aulete's piped song," the "silvery sea" with their oars.[5] Yet they may have been moving to threaten, as Thucydides tells us, the Melians with utter ruin unless they submitted to the Athenian empire.[6] And in Roman times those triremes would be manned by slaves, moving in perfect synchrony to the whips' lash and the beat of drums. Or consider the Nuremberg Rally of 1934, orchestrated to perfection by Albert Speer and preserved for posterity on film by Leni Riefenstahl. These were instruments of power, but they aimed for and achieved a kind of beauty. On an entirely different tack, the psalms often describe God's law as a delight to the soul and perfect submission to it as our highest good. Perhaps, however, that submission is a willing, acknowledging, and judging submission, like an orchestra's submission to its conductor.

There is not, then, a *necessary* connection between beauty and justice—at least if justice requires respect for other men's liberty. Still, Scarry's thesis is haunting. Perhaps beauty that grows out of evil and injustice is tainted and mocks, as it enchants those who enjoy it. Think of the slavery, misery, and death visited by the con-quistadors, whose American gold was used to adorn the ceiling of Santa Maria Maggiore. Nor is the deprivation of liberty visited only on those who must pay for the beauty; it is also visited on those who perform it, as in the case of the sublime music issuing from the voices of the Italian *castrati* in earlier centuries. If sex with a beautiful woman can be counted as an enjoyment of beauty, then what about the sultan's harem? These are extravagant examples. A Wal-Mart–free Vermont is more ordinary but also shows how some people are willing to sacrifice the liberty of others to assure the beauty of the Vermont landscape and townscape.

Beauty is a relatively benign example of the goods for which people have been ready to sacrifice other people's liberty. (I do not mean the loss of liberty that willing recruits undergo, for that may be counted an exercise—perverse, perhaps—of liberty rather than its sacrifice.) The glory of a family, tribe, race, nation, or religion has been the most virulent. Glory is beauty magnified exponentially—a resplendence. And in its name, mountains of corpses and miles of chains have built up over the centuries, making the sacrifice of liberty for glory among the lesser horrors perpetrated in its name. Yet it is important, and not just because liberty is our subject, but because to modern minds there is something paradoxical about sacrificing liberty to so immaterial a goal as glory. Coerced adherence, wonder, admiration, reverence, prostration, seem counterfeits of these responses freely experienced. But that is a mistake. First of all, when the Aztec priest cuts open the breast of his victim and seizes the beating heart, it is not to amaze the victim but rather to amaze the audience. So the parade of captives following a general in his triumph provided delight, pride, confirmation of a sense of superiority to the Roman population that witnessed the spectacle. To the captives it was, and was meant to be, an ultimate humiliation—*invidens/privata deduci superbo/non humilis mulier triumpho.*[7] Their humiliation was part of the general's and his compatriots' glory. But more pertinently, in some religions and creeds, forced adherence, reluctant obeisance—for example, the pinch of incense that subject peoples were required to offer before the altar of the Roman gods—added to the glory of the gods. Free mental assent, liberty, were not the point: the clenched teeth, the coercion, added to the show of power.

The Good of Liberty

Is the case for liberty like that? We have been told that it is. Some men, some societies, pursue beauty or glory, others liberty. This presents liberty as one goal among others, a competitor for our attention. But is not liberty different in kind from the other things that men and nations value? Liberty is a relation in which I stand to other men, albeit a negative one: they may ignore but they may not purposefully hinder me. Liberty is like an adverb qualifying how we pursue other goods—for instance, beauty. And being negative—the absence of other men's purposefully hindering me—it can be present in everything we do. But is it, as beauty is, an end in itself? Scarry makes beauty adverbial too, arguing that many of life's goals can be pursued beautifully—in a way that creates beauty. But still beauty is more naturally seen as an end in itself, and one to which other ends are often sacrificed. It is not merely adverbial. Many things are done for the sake of their beauty alone, but with liberty, everything done freely is done for some other reason too. There is no such thing as liberty apart from the things we are at liberty to do. The adverb without the verb can never make a complete moral sentence—a complete idea—except as a provisional abstraction, waiting to be attached to something.

In all these examples the liberty (and much more) of some is sacrificed for the goals of others. Yet these are all goals that may be and often are chosen freely. In even my most awful examples, someone has freely chosen the goal that makes so many others miserable. Someone has exercised his liberty to deprive others of theirs. Thus, in a sense liberty is its own competitor.

Should not a rational, striving man always be willing to consider trading some degree of liberty for the sake of one or more of the things he strives for? I can imagine a man so devoted to beauty—or the service and glory of his family, nation, or gods— that he will sacrifice any amount of all other things he truly values to enjoy beauty, or *ad maiorem Dei gloriam*. Is it even coherent to imagine the man who wishes to be free in the pursuit of his goods but refuses to give up some of his liberty in order to attain those goods? After all, do I not sacrifice (if that is the word) my liberty to play the piano this hour by reading poetry instead? Does not the natural athlete sacrifice his potential as a runner by devoting himself to swimming?

This fallacious objection reminds us what liberty is. When I choose one thing rather than another, this is not a sacrifice of my liberty. It is its exercise. Only when *someone else* forces me to choose one goal rather than another is my liberty compromised. As long as I do the choosing, there is no issue for liberty; as soon as another forces me to choose—even among goods I greatly value—my liberty is to that extent gone. I emphasize this to sharpen the terms of the competition between liberty and other goods. Beauty, the glory of my tribe, service to humanity, the passion for equality, do not compete with liberty—they compete *with each other* for how I will exercise my liberty.

What if a dictatorial family or regime offers me the opportunity to pursue some goal I value and would have chosen above all others on my own, so long as I agree to give up my liberty in other regards? This is the "freedom" enjoyed by scientists and artists under Stalin and by entrepreneurs in twenty-first-century Shanghai, the political power and freedom enjoyed by high eunuch courtiers in the Ottoman Empire and by every employee who is allowed more or less discretion and initiative but only so long as he advances the employer's goals. Sometimes such restrictions are accepted exactly in the spirit of exercising one's liberty, as in the case of a scholar who accepts the mild restraints of university policies and obligations in order to pursue his research. At other times, as in the Soviet and Ottoman examples, this seems too Pollyannaish an account, but only because in one kind of example we may accept that those who impose have a right to exercise their liberty by conditioning their cooperation in certain ways, while in the other examples the imposition is unjust and tyrannical and so the choice it leaves is also tyrannical.

What is a just or unjust imposition will be a principal concern of later chapters. For the moment, I ask you to accept that both just and unjust impositions, fair and unfair choices, are presented to us. If the choice is a fair one—one that the imposer is entitled to face me with—then to insist on my liberty in the case of that choice is in fact to impose on the liberty of the other person. These are difficult lines, but they must be drawn. Where I am faced with such a justified choice, it is not a question of liberty, any more than the choice to eat less and exercise more in order to reach a healthy weight is. So what is so good about liberty if in any event I must continually give up one thing in order to get another? Is the value of liberty anything other than the value of the goods between which I must choose? Or, to put it another way, if we take one by one the value of the choices I have to make, is the sum of the net value of all the goods I can choose (net, because I must be willing to pay the price of dieting, of moving to another city) not exactly equivalent to the value of my liberty? Or, to put it still another way, if I get everything I would get whether or not I am a free man, is there any value left over just from being free?[8]

Liberty is worth more than just the sum of the goods we are not prevented from attaining. I am free to the extent that I can choose my good. I may be happy without choice. I may enjoy some goods without having chosen them, but a life without choice, a life consisting of unchosen goods, is an inhuman existence—or if it is human, it is human in the way of a baby in its mother's womb. Any attempt to explain this bedrock notion risks banality. One part of such an explanation is the evident fact that what counts as good for us changes as a result of the choices we make. Another is that the choices we make of our good are the result of reflection, and not just of reflection about how best to achieve a given good. Reason is not only the slave of the passions; sometimes it channels or arouses passion.

Immanuel Kant has shown how reflection leads us to see that regard for humanity in our own person and the person of others requires us to accept certain constraints on our choices; these are the constraints of morality, and recognizing them, we come not just to accept and live according to them but to love them as a good. Reflection leads us to respect humanity in our own person and in the person of others, and that respect becomes a source of satisfaction in itself. In much the same vein John Rawls, after developing an elaborate argument for the constraints that a just society must accept and impose on its members in the pursuit of particular goods, in the most moving portion of his great work, *A Theory of Justice*, doubles back to show that in a just society, justice itself comes to be loved as a good.[9] All this simply points to the bedrock notion that it is impossible to excavate without breaking our expository spades: that as human beings we do not just experience good and evil but reflect upon and choose them, that goods not chosen are hardly human at all—though perhaps they may be divine, falling upon us as heavenly grace.[10] It follows that when we are deprived of our power of choice, we are not just infantilized, we are dehumanized, whatever good things are returned to us in exchange.

Liberty and Respect

So liberty, like glory, pleasure, ease, and beauty, is not just an instrument; it is a particular kind of good in itself. And as with glory, pleasure, and beauty, do not men seek and increase their liberty by violating the liberty of others? The nineteenth-century North Atlantic middle classes enjoyed great liberty of thought and action, but on the backs of oppressed colonial masses. There is, however, a connection between the value of liberty for me and of liberty for you. I have explained that liberty is only implicated if others try to deprive me of choice, not if they simply fail to help me or fail to get out of my way, and certainly not if my choices are limited by impersonal circumstances, even drastically, as by death. The aptness of this conception of liberty may now come clearer. Of course I can only plan according to—choose between—what the world offers me. Indeed, planning and choosing are about fitting my plans into the world as it is. The man who deliberately deprives me of choice, who manipulates my choices, manipulates me. He does not ignore, as does the indifferent man, my human capacity for choice; he addresses it and addresses it in order to diminish it. He disrespects me. (Think of Iago's manipulation of Othello.) The implication I draw follows from what I have argued liberty is: it is a relation among people. It is a relation in which each person refrains from interfering with the self-determination of others. It is a relation in which people respect each other—in a limited way, to be sure: they do not necessarily help each other get what they want or need; they do not necessarily love or even like each other. But they do respect each other—or, to put it in a brief if circular way, they respect each other's liberty.

This idea of respect and disrespect gains force from its next iteration. Here are three ways to relate to other persons: disregard, disrespect, and their opposite, unasked-for generosity. These are not the most important. The most important is respect. So far I have given only a negative account of that relation of respect: it is when another deliberately forbears from depriving me of choice. But the positive aspect is far more important. That comes in when another involves himself in my liberty not to hinder but to further my choices—as choices, not as the unasked-for gifts from heaven. Often he will do this for a reason: because it will further *his* choices. He helps me so I will help him; I help him so he will help me. Most of the things we want we cannot get by ourselves; we need the help of others. We can get that help in ways that respect or disrespect them. When we collaborate freely, we make two kinds of things: whatever it is we are building and the fellowship of collaboration itself. Just as liberty is a good over and above the particular goods we freely choose, so collaboration is a good over and above the goods we collaborate in creating. And just like liberty itself, the fellowship of collaboration opens new vistas for choice, suggests new goods to choose. This is the beau ideal. But even slavery is a kind of collaboration: the master feeds the slave and refrains from beating him in return for the slave's entire service. And then there is what the Marxists called wage slavery. To keep the ideal from covering too much, or nothing at all, we need to mark the difference between what another may offer, threaten, or refuse while respecting my liberty and what offers, threats, and refusals violate it. It is the line between my rights and the rights of another. Marking that line is liberty's most difficult intellectual task. I begin to address it in this chapter, but only after considering liberty's closest competitor.

Equality

Everything is what it is: liberty is liberty, not equality or fairness or justice or culture, or human happiness or a quiet conscience. . . . If I curtail or lose my freedom in order to lessen the shame of such inequality (in a particular society), and do not thereby materially increase the individual liberty of others, an absolute loss of liberty occurs. To think otherwise is a confusion of values.[11]

Equality is liberty's closest competitor and nearest relative. It is a manifold and elusive concept, like liberty itself. We have asked and continually will ask, Liberty to do what, when, and why? In a like way we ask, Equality of what, and measured how? Liberty and equality are in a sense both adverbial—we pursue other goals freely or enjoy them equally. It is not surprising that the two ideas often wear each other's dress, or that some have even said there is no such thing as one of them, only the other.

The first two examples with which I began this book, the Quebec Charter of the French Language and the Canada Health system, have been justified in the name of equality. Quebec's health-care system bars the exits not in order to give the best possible care to some, however selected, but in order to give the best possible care to all alike, consistent with overall budget constraints. Whether the average level of care is higher than in the United States is debatable; what is clear is that some people in the United States—because of their wealth, or where they live, or the kind of insurance their employers carry—get better care than the average in either place. Quebec's health-care system is designed to prevent that. I have suggested one explanation behind this pressure for what is called equal access: to improve the overall health of the population by giving everyone a stake in the system, so that the most powerful and the best informed know that the only way they can improve their care is to raise the level for everybody. But that is too sophisticated a political calculation to enlist the loyalty of a whole society. The exits are barred in the name of equality, of community.

Equality expresses the notion that we are all in the same boat, that we all have the same moral worth. It is one way—only one—of expressing the bond of community. An army too can be a community, though the furthest thing from a community of equality, except in the sense that all share (perhaps equally) the common goal of victory and are equally prepared to sacrifice even their lives, certainly their material equality, to that shared goal. Community and equality are correlated notions. Churches and states are communities; an army is just another, different example. These communities may be devoted to a variety of goals, including beauty and glory. If their members pursue these goals and accept their discipline freely, there is no problem about liberty—except as they impose, as they often do, on others outside the community. But in liberal democratic states like Canada, equality and the concomitant community may be a goal in themselves. The state is liberal insofar as individual citizens are free to pursue their own chosen goals. In this way it is not like a church or an army or Mussolini's ideal fascist state, which Yeats so admired. Yet an egalitarian liberal community does have a common purpose, a shared ideal that not only constrains but trumps the individual goals of its members. That common purpose is equality itself—and the community that equality expresses and creates.

The Equal Worth of Persons

Behind the embrace of equality as an ultimate end is a conception of the worth of persons. Persons are infinitely various in appearance, individual and group history, capacity, disposition, wishes, and desires, but there is that which they all share, that which makes them count as persons, and all of those differences are overwhelmed by that shared character, which has been variously described. The most primitive description is simply what might be called phenotypic: all who look human—that is, look like you and me?—are human. Obvious trouble lurks in such a notion: women do not look exactly like men, dark-skinned persons are different in that regard from lighter-skinned, and what of dwarves? It is a logic that has ended in some of the cruelest and most inhuman practices in history. And of course there is here no principle at all; any differentiating feature of appearance may be—and has been—seized on to exclude some from the circle of community. Lincoln made this point eloquently in 1854:

> If A. can prove, however conclusively, that he may, of right, enslave B.—why may not B. snatch the same argument, and prove equally, that he may enslave A?—
>
> You say A. is white, and B. is black. It is *color*, then; the lighter, having the right to enslave the darker? Take care. By this rule, you are to be slave to the first man you meet, with a fairer skin than your own.
>
> You do not mean *color* exactly?—You mean the whites are *intellectually* the superior of the blacks, and, therefore, have the right to enslave them? Take care again. By this rule, you are to be slave to the first man you meet, with an intellect superior to your own.
>
> But, say you, it is a question of *interest*; and, if you can make it your interest, you have the right to enslave another. Very well. And if he can make it his interest, he has the right to enslave you.[12]

The deep objection to such ways of drawing the boundaries is that they do not explain why those included and those excluded deserve different treatment. The tightest circle of all is drawn just around me, but that small circle cannot be offered to others as a reason why I should be treated with consideration and respect but they should not. The inclusions and exclusions do not describe a moral argument at all. They all boil down to a larger or narrower circle of solipsism. As in all forms of solipsism, the solipsist says, "I know what I know, and refuse to offer evidence or argument; I prefer myself and exclude you, and refuse to give a reason." As the solipsist declines to give you reasons, to offer evidence, he simply declines to recognize you at all—to converse with you, to enter into the minimal community of discourse with you. Solipsism is contrary to reason; it denies reason.

I reject solipsism because it denies reason, judgment. I have identified reason and judgment as what makes us individuals, persons. In recognizing myself as a locus of reason and judgment—my reason, my judgment—I make a claim for my status as an individual, a claim on you. In making that claim on you, I cannot without solipsism, without unreason, deny you that same status. Here is a kind of equality: we are both reasoning, judging beings. Since the Enlightenment, this course of argument has taken two forms. The utilitarians—in the slogan "Each to count for one, none for more than one"—have focused on the capacity to feel pain and pleasure as the bond and basis for equality, because they see pain and pleasure (pain and pleasure of all sorts, higher and lower, as Mill emphasized) as all there is of value.[13] It is that capacity which gives individuals (including, to a greater or lesser degree, animals) a claim on each other's concern. The concern varies only with the capacity of each to feel pleasure and pain.

The second account, the one I affirm, is associated with Kant but really goes back much further. The capacity for judgment, to make plans, to choose one's good, is what we share with other persons. It is what makes us persons. (Some would have it that dogs, dolphins, and apes share this capacity to some extent.[14] If it is so, so be it.) It is what makes possible the forms of collaboration that are distinctly human: speech, argument, the offering of reasons and evidence, cooperation, laws, cultures, civilizations, histories. I therefore (therefore!) owe respect and equal respect to all who share this capacity, and they owe it to me. Here too is a basis for the principle of equality: for whether another is male or female, strong or weak, young or old, intelligent or not, of my clan, nation, or family or not, he still has that capacity. (There are difficulties I shall not pursue about the very young, the unconscious, the mentally impaired, and perhaps those incapable of recognizing anything in common with others—what might be called moral idiots.)[15] It is an equality of moral capacity—what Kant called freedom and reason. It is an equality in precisely that aspect of our persons that allows us to make judgments about what we should choose, what I have identified as the soul of individuality. The argument is circular; it circles over the truth about what makes us persons and what makes us valuable as persons. It is profoundly individualistic: however much we choose to pursue goods in common, however much we value others, we start from the fact of our own individual choosing. That is the conception of persons, of individuality, of morality that I embrace.[16]

This conception is profoundly egalitarian. Is it egalitarian in the same way that the Charter of the French Language and Quebec's health-care system are? Start with a caricature: It is said that in Sweden, parents at one time were forbidden to pay for music lessons or hire tutors for their children. These things were available in the system of public education and in good supply and quality, but in the name of equality parents could not use their discretionary income to advance their children above what the public system would provide. Although the distribution of income in Sweden is much more equal than in many advanced democracies, many persons have a significant amount of discretionary income; whatever advantages higher-income or thriftier families may enjoy, this rule works against making those advantages heritable.[17] Such a practice, even less ambiguously than the three examples with which I began this book, firmly sacrifices liberty to equality. The parents (or the child, if old enough) enjoy no more income than this rigorously egalitarian society allows, so there is no question of taking anything away from anyone else. This is a

kind of educational sumptuary law. Imagine if adults were forbidden from using their discretionary income to buy, or even in their
leisure time to make, brighter, more beautiful clothes than their
fellow citizens wear. Or if women were discouraged from using
their ingenuity and talents to cultivate their looks so as to be more
beautiful. It would be clearer still, I suppose, if adults were prevented from reading, traveling, conversing—thinking?—in ways
that would make them livelier and more interesting, their lives, if
not their bank accounts, richer. I do not make this up. Think of
Pol Pot. There have always been societies that have accomplished
such things by informal but also by formal rule.

Societies that have preached and enforced equality by raising
the depths if possible but by lowering the heights if need be are
as salient and maybe as numerous as those dedicated to glory,
beauty, truth, or the cultivation of virtue. You might protest that
I describe a rule not of equality but of envy—that passion which
would rather see men chopped down than have any rise above
the mean. But what is the difference between the passion that
we call envy and a passion for equality that goes so far as to prefer that some have less even if their excess takes nothing from
anyone else? Think how hard I have had to work to explain that
my three examples are not really driven by envy. If I have not altogether convinced you, it may be because you suspect that envy
is at work there after all. But to dismiss this passion for equality
as envy is to argue by epithet. If it is envy to lop the tops off trees
that stand too tall, then envy is just another word for a passion
for equality, and equality for a passion for justice. Is there not
even a kind of beauty in equality? Here is Scarry again, quoting
Saint Augustine:

> The higher things are those in which equality resides, supreme,
> unshaken, unchangeable, eternal. . . .

Beautiful things please by proportion . . . equality is not found only in sounds for the ear and in bodily movements, but also in visible forms, in which hitherto equality has been identified with beauty even more customarily than in sounds.[18]

So not only in Pol Pot's egalitarian hell but everywhere equality can appear as liberty's most potent rival. Is not my argument at war with itself? I have argued that my individual responsibility for my judgments and choices is what is most important to me and that from this idea of my personality follows the transcendent importance to me of my liberty, of my not being the tool of another, subject to another. I have also insisted that this very moral core of my personality is present in equal measure in every person, so that the argument by which my liberty must be respected requires me to respect equally. But finally—to complete my circle of apparent self-contradiction—I have given example after example where liberty is confined, sometimes violently, in the name of equality.

Equal Liberty

The way out is clear and classic. It is indeed the case that respect for the liberty of each individual follows from what is most important about us as persons, and that this pertains to all of us equally just because we are persons. What follows is not that equality trumps liberty but rather that what is owed each of us is *equal liberty*. More specifically, we are all owed *the greatest measure of liberty compatible with a like liberty for all*.[19] Think of an older (unrelated) argument: what is most important about each of us is that we are each God's creatures, made in His image, and this fact is so overwhelming that it trumps any differences between us—rich or poor, man or woman, Jew or Gentile. But what follows is not Pol Pot, nor that equality is the first good for humans, but rather our equality as creatures of God. In just that way we all can claim a maximum of liberty. If attaining equality along some other measure—say, health, education, or wealth in general—requires unequal respect for the liberty of some relative to others, then this is not justified. Nor is it justified to achieve equality by eliminating (or squeezing down) everybody's liberty equally. What we are due is the *greatest* liberty compatible with a like liberty for all. It is neither the equality of the graveyard nor that of the universal prison.

This is a grand principle. What does it mean? What is this greatest liberty, and how can we tell when it is enjoyed equally by all? Liberty, as I have identified and distinguished it from other things we value, is an absence. It is an absence of restraints purposely placed on me by others and especially by governments. It is not, recall, the same as my ability to get all the things I want; nor is it the same as having others (the government) remove obstacles in my path or help me to get what I want. I may have a right to government's or my neighbor's help, but that claim is not about liberty. So it should be easy: the greatest equal liberty is when each of us goes about his business without interfering with or being interfered with by another, except as we choose to ask for or give our cooperation. We may be unequal in everything that we care about—health, satisfaction of our desires, the ability to advance and comfort our friends and family. Still it may be easy to say we are equal in our liberty, in our freedom from imposition by others.

Too easy. Am I really at liberty if others so press about me that I can hardly move, even if they are not trying to hinder me—they just will not get out of my way as they go about their business?

Oliver Wendell Holmes said that my freedom to swing my fist ends at the tip of your nose.[20] At the least, should we not accept something like the rules of the road, as they will help all of us get wherever we want to go more quickly and surely? Although this involves restrictions on liberty—purposeful ones, at that—is it not a restriction consistent with the greatest liberty of all? This seems reasonable, but the details do not quite work. The benign-sounding "rules of the road" comes closer to meeting my definition of infringements of liberty than do any of the actions in the chaos they are designed to regulate. The man who drives down the middle of the highway heedless of those to the left and the right of him is just that, heedless, while the state trooper and the rules he enforces have me and my choices directly in their sights. Yet we are glad to have the trooper there to keep both me and other drivers in line. So in this simplest of examples we seem quite ready to trade away a bit of liberty (our own and that of our fellow travelers) against a measure of assurance that we will be better able to get to our various destinations. I will dwell for a while on this benign example to see whether it does not lead eventually to the perhaps more sinister ones with which I began this book—not to mention Pol Pot.

Liberty and Cooperation

It is easier to think of the rules of the road as a cooperative project than to claim acceptance that way for the Charter of the French Language. If all of us who use the highway were to meet— perhaps after a spell of quite terrible accidents—might we not agree that those traveling west use the north side of the highway, those east the south? We might even paint a stripe down the middle to make clear what was north and south. In any situation such as this one, it is hard to imagine why anyone would not agree. The road hog would then be disregarding not only fellow travelers but his own agreement with them. May we force those who have agreed to keep to their bargain without violating their liberty? Notice that such compulsion would no longer just be a matter of refusing to take account of others, which is what the man who drives down the middle of the road does in respect to others on the road. No, here we would take exactly the kind of focused, purposeful action that implicates the road hog's liberty. The reason this might be all right must be that he has agreed to the system he now threatens to spoil. The agreement makes the difference.

Choice inevitably means forfeiting alternative choices; we show no disrespect to ourselves as free persons, we do not offend against our own liberty, by making choices. Indeed, to refuse to make choices is to abandon the use of the very liberty I have been celebrating, and it cannot be that liberty is valuable only if not used. Why does not my agreement count as just such a use of my liberty? Is it because the restriction of opportunities may not take place right away, as it does when I turn south rather than north? (Yogi Berra: "When you come to a fork in the road, take it!") Why should that matter? There are many quite personal choices I make that restrict my liberty—visit their consequences on me— only after some delay, as when I smoke, knowing that years later my health will be ruined.

The narrowing of options associated with agreeing to the lane division is, however, not like the lung cancer and emphysema in my smoking example. Should it make a difference that the restriction on choice comes about not through impersonal forces but rather through the focused intervention of others? To make anything turn on that, to see in this a restriction (or at least a wrongful restriction) on liberty, would be to put systematically beyond reach the most important—and the most human—use of our liberty: where we join with others as free persons freely to pursue some shared or complementary goals (recall my earlier example of the collaboration of Mozart and his librettist, da Ponte).

So just as there is some special harm when a man not only runs over me or passes me by but looks me in the eye and uses me, deprives me of my liberty for his ends, so there is an extra measure, a *creative* measure of respect when we "use" each other freely in the way of collaboration. (This might be an example of what Hegel thought of as the opposition of thesis and antithesis being brought together in a synthesis to take us to a higher level—here of liberty.) And of course the coordination that agreement makes possible is not limited to instant, simultaneous exchanges: a trade, pulling together on a rope, love. Our freedom and rationality, our judgment and understanding, will be most intricately, most humanly implicated when our joint program takes place over time and with many steps. (An orchestra playing together exhibits both intricately time-extended and simultaneous coordination of effort.)

It is a long way from actual, small-scale, face-to-face instances of free collaboration to Quebec's health-care system and Wal-Mart—or the system of property law, criminal law, income taxes. Philosophers (Locke, Kant, Rawls) have offered a number of ways to get from the individual or small-scale collaboration to the great impersonal processes of the state. Many of these offer some insight; none have been proof against objections as ingenious as the arguments themselves. I shall not add to this literature. I shall go instead directly to the question of what laws and institutions most reasonably accord with *the principle of the greatest equal liberty* (the principle of liberty, for short), assuming along the way that there must be government, there must be laws.

My brief discussion of the rules of the road and of the compatibility of enforceable agreements with the principle of liberty is not intended as a stand-in for a general account of the origin of the state. These are rather examples of the kinds of arrangements, institutions, laws that meet the test of the principle of liberty. And they point to two general institutions that always have been—for good reason—associated with, and thought to be necessary to, a regime of liberty: property and contract. Is it possible to give an account of property and contract as based in and supporting the principle of liberty? Or are even these most basic institutions vulnerable to the claims of liberty's competitors: the power and glory of factions on one end and equality (not equal liberty) on the other? More succinctly, that inquiry will ask, Is liberty possible?[21]

CHAPTER 3

LIBERTY
AND RIGHTS

Telling a man what he may or may not do restricts his liberty. All my examples have been of government telling people what to do. Is liberty, then, only about what government does to us, not what we do to each other? And, more fundamentally, is liberty just an absence of restraints imposed by someone, so that a broken leg, a downed bridge, and even gravity do not count as restrictions on our liberty?

Philosophers, like ordinary people, speak of liberty in many contexts and senses. There is the liberty of the person free from desires and impulses. And none of us are free as a bird, to rise up from our places and fly. Closer to my concerns is the liberty I do not have to cruise on a yacht I do not own, to cure my sick child with medicines I cannot get. And, going back to the examples in the first chapter, I am not free to conduct my Quebec business in English, to set up a private, fee-only clinic in Quebec, or to open a Wal-Mart in the National Trust's vision for Vermont.

Liberty is about how others use me. It is not about my abstract ability to do what I want—fly to the moon, marry the girl of my dreams. If my ability to do what I want is limited because others are in my way or because they will not help me get where I am going, I cannot reasonably feel that those others are *using* me. It may be more like their refusing to let me use *them*, although to be sure I may have a reasonable complaint that they inhumanely or cruelly disregard my interests. Think of the difference between the man who ties me up and the man who, coming upon me tied, will not untie me. From one perspective—that of my actual capabilities, what I can do—my liberty is equally limited in both instances, but only the first man deprives me of my liberty.[1]

This is more than a point of terminology. Liberty is a relation between persons in a way that a focus on my capabilities need not be. A world that puts capability first is one that may call on persons—individuals!—to modify, align, even sacrifice their liberty so that others enjoy some measure—equal or minimal, however measured—of freedom, as capability. Liberty is not like that. We may all enjoy a full measure of liberty without subtracting from the liberty of anyone else. This is one way in which liberty expresses our separateness from each other. It is the same separateness that I have identified as the basic, indigestible fact of our individuality. There are other dimensions to my life with others: what help I can count on; what relations of love and friendship I can enjoy; what products of the liberty of others I can enjoy—in sum, what kind of social world I live in. But liberty is distinct from these.

So far I have only argued what liberty is and why it is distinct and important. Are you convinced? Why not? Is it because you are still inclined to think that what really counts is whether a man reaches his goals, feels the satisfactions that his goals bring him, and that whether his liberty has been interfered with or respected along the way does not matter, or at least matters no more than whether others have failed to help him or got out of his way in attaining those goals, those satisfactions? You are wrong. What gives my goals and satisfactions worth—depth and intensity—is that they are mine, that I have imagined them, seen them, judged and chosen them. One might say that this is why they are the goals and satisfactions of a person with a soul—not a machine or just an organism, an animal. Our self-reflective perception, our judging and choosing, are what constitute our soul, our consciousness, our conscience (sometimes). Liberty recognizes my soul and asks whether and how others recognize my soul too, recognize me as a person. So freedom in the sense of capability is a very general notion that includes the animal and the solitary; liberty is about personal relationships, that is, relations between persons.

You violate my liberty when you interfere with me. But you might interfere with me not deliberately but just because I get in your way. If you push me away or run me over, you do not use me; you disregard me. Is that like gravity, under the influence of which I am a mere physical object, unthinking and unknowing? If it is, then do I violate your liberty when I ward you off as you come at me, not because you care to do me harm but just because you do not care about me at all as you head toward your goal? After all, I do exactly that with a tree branch falling across my path. Notice the asymmetry: when you would run me over, you do not necessarily interfere with me *deliberately*, but when I ward you off, I do. Can it be that you respect (or do not disrespect) my liberty but I violate yours?

The Rights Bubble

Imagine that each of us moves through life surrounded by a bubble. If someone enters my bubble unbidden, I do not invade his liberty—his bubble—by repelling that invasion. But the contours of the bubble are conceptual and not just spatial. If you and I are both out on the highway on a stormy day and you skid into me, there is a perfectly straightforward sense in which I have invaded your space just as much as you have invaded mine, and perhaps neither of our situations should be seen in those terms. (Holmes also said that even a dog distinguishes between being stumbled over and being kicked.)[2] And the contours are more intricate even than that. If you blunder into me unawares, perhaps I can push you away, but if I shoot you dead, I had better be able to show that this was the only way I could protect myself from comparable harm. From the basic idea that liberty means a person is not available to be used by me, we have had to move to the idea that I may use another after all, but only defensively, even when I am defending against dangers that the other person does not mean to threaten me with. If I could not maneuver among my fellow actors without wronging them, then my liberty might well be worthless—and theirs too.

Having started with liberty as an idea about people's unavailability to be used, that is, being tampered with deliberately, we have come to include considerations of unintended impingements—what I first called others running over or disregarding me. But that was to take account of the fact that I may deliberately impinge on another after all without violating his liberty, if I do so defensively and in due measure. In this way the notion of liberty—not being used by others—is correlated with the notion of right, or of rights. I have no right to use another or he to use me. But I do have a right to defend against his violation of my rights. The many-dimensional contours of my bubble (not just space-time, but what we might call moral or liberty space) trace the extent of my rights. This is the moral space I inhabit; I am morally secure within it. No one may trespass upon it without doing me wrong. Because it is mine—because these are my rights—I can also invite others in. I can venture out of my space to visit others who invite me into theirs. My friend does not use me if she enters my space invited, so that we can dance together there. Nor does she violate my liberty if I tell her to bring her friends so we can all have a party.

From Property to Contract

What I describe, of course, is property: property in my person, in the space about me, and . . . what else? If property extends not only to a bubble around my own person but also to certain objects outside me—which, as I shall show, it does—then it is also my right to trade parts of it away. I can lend it—and then the borrower violates my rights when he does not give it back and I do not violate his when I take it back. To see how fertile this set of notions is—and remember, they are all generated by the basic idea of liberty—consider this: We do a trade. I give you a wonderfully soft, broad-brimmed felt hat in return for one of your exquisite carvings. But you have not made the carving yet, and you want my hat right now. The scope of both of our liberties would be narrowed— our bubbles would shrink—if there were no way for me to give you the hat now while being sure of getting the carving you have offered me in return. Our bubbles would shrink, and no one else's would be larger. This would be a general and pointless contraction of human liberty. (Recall that I have spoken of equal *maxi-*

mum liberty—the greatest liberty compatible with a like liberty for all.) So the contours of my right are drawn along the dimension of time: your future property in the carving is now mine, but only as future property. This is what a promise does: it makes your future performance my present right.[3] If, when the carving is finally made, you do not hand it over to me, you violate my rights as surely as if it were already in my bubble and you had marched in and taken it from me.

From Liberty to Law

I have described the rudiments of the concepts of property and contract. Children seem to understand the concepts of promise and property early on; property and contract are everywhere legal institutions, institutions of the state.[4] In trying to get to the bottom of what liberty is, we seem to have moved very quickly from a general (and generous) idea of liberty to the state, which is often the greatest enemy of liberty—and if not that enemy, the place where liberty's greatest enemies lurk. If liberty works itself out— among other things—in regimes of property and contract, and if property and contract depend on law (that is, the state), are we then stuck with only as much liberty as the state gives us? Or, even worse, is whatever the state gives us in fact liberty, for that reason alone? The move from liberty to the state went too fast.

We might have property and contract without the state. There might be ideas about the size and shape of our multidimensional bubble without the state or any of its laws, and there might also be ideas about when we have made agreements with each other that should be honored. Let us call these ideas about our rights. These ideas may be quite widely held. And if there are such widely held ideas, the state would enter the picture for a number of very important but merely practical reasons. First, though many may agree, not all will respect the bounds of our property and honor their contracts unless they are made to do it. In the same vein, things may come to such a pass that so many violate our property and dishonor their undertakings that hardly anybody will any longer respect and perform agreements unless everybody is made to. This happens in societies that have descended into anarchy—say, after losing a war—and accounts for the degradation of their economy. Second, many of us might agree about what our rights are in a general way but disagree at various levels of particularity as to what those rights are. For instance, we might all agree that our bubbles entitle us to move down a common road, but only on one or the other side. There is no way that we can decide whether we should drive on the left or the right just by thinking about it harder, because no one cares which side we choose and everyone cares that the matter be settled. We might all agree about the importance of keeping our promises, but there may be a dispute about whether someone has actually made a promise on a particular occasion. In the first instance we speak of legislation, in the second of adjudication. (Legislation and adjudication shade into each other, but nothing turns on that here.)

It is generally thought that we must have the state for enforcement, legislation, and adjudication, and that is why rights (property and contract) are creatures of the state. But that is a non sequitur. It is entirely plausible to argue that we have the rights we have whether or not they are enforced, embodied in codes, or officially adjudicated. Indeed, that is what I believe, and perhaps you do too. Our rights—not all of them, nor in all their detail, but in their broad outlines—are the entailments of what we are: free and reasoning persons, capable of a conception of what is good and right, so that in the end we are urgently responsible to our-

selves for achieving that good (which in all likelihood often concerns the good of others). It is because our rights flow from who
and what we are that we may form, re-form, or accept states in
order to make our rights more certain and secure. So those who
say that our rights depend on or are the creatures of states have it
the wrong way around.

The obvious difficulty in this account—the one the enemies
of liberty make their heartiest meal of—is that it really is only an
account about generalities: there may well be a pre-law (pre-
state) *notion* that we have rights and that respecting our liberty
means respecting those rights. That pre-law notion may be conceded to extend to cover the free exchange of rights. And so there
might be a vibrant pre-law notion that we do have rights, that we
have a right to "our" property—in our persons and in our things—
and that we have the right to have contracts (that is, trades, gifts,
promises) about our rights honored. What we cannot get to on our
own, without laws and so without a state, is the content and
details of those rights. And rights without content are empty. Liberty means honoring our rights, and if the content of our rights is
only what the state says it is, then while the *general idea* of rights,
and the *general idea* of liberty may be secure against the state, the
substance of each depends entirely on the state after all.[5] This is
a difficulty that has to be confronted, but first let me see how far
we can get on energy generated by the general idea alone.

Markets: The Community of Liberty

Allowing free trades on open markets, in an argument made
famous by Adam Smith, increases efficiency and maximizes individual welfare by channeling resources to their highest and best

use. But a free market is not just an instrument and engine of efficiency, it is the crossroads where two or more—usually many more—people using their liberty come together. In my conception, markets are what I would call the community of liberty. In recent years something of an intellectual scandal has been caused by economics-minded scholars who have analyzed such apparently noncommercial interactions among people as courtship and adoption. The study of markets for art (sometimes called patronage) is so familiar and long-standing that it does not alarm sensibilities in the way that talk of "markets" for (or the "economics" of) affection, sex, and spontaneous generosity does. But it is a failure of imagination and clear thinking to treat human interactions in which shoes, construction work, and the like are exchanged, directly or for money, as radically distinct from interactions involving art, love, and human caring. The propagandist sees the latter as more elevated, perhaps sublime, the former as banal and low. But this mistaken view does not elevate love and art so much as it wrongly devalues work and trade. In both love and trade, human beings use their liberty and elicit some corresponding use of their freedom from those with whom they interact.

Does this account leave out acts of pure generosity? Of course these exist and can be wonderful, but the temptation to overdo the special value of generosity also is a kind of devaluing (or denaturing) of the kinds of interactions we value most. The mother's selfless care for her infant elicits a smile of recognition, the beginning of a mutual relation, of collaboration. And collaboration is an especially human exercise of liberty, a manifestation of human personality—perhaps the highest. Think of a chamber quartet playing in ensemble: every nuance of tone, every gesture and look, elicits and guides a reciprocal response. It is but a prejudice—and an impoverishing one at that—to miss similar reciprocity in what are sometimes deprecated as "mere" market exchanges. To be sure, there are differences between candy, shoes, music, and love: each is higher and more valuable than the other. These may even be different in kind—that is not my point. My point is to emphasize how, up and down the range, these values present opportunities for human interaction, and these interactions may be the manifestations of free persons freely using their liberty. Why be surprised that the products of such collaborations—art, science, cities, and churches—should be among the greatest monuments of man's passage on this planet?

There have been many objections to this conception, some born of misunderstanding and prejudice. There is the complaint that goes under the nonsense tag "commodification." By joining art and love together with buying and selling, we debase the former, wrongly exalt the latter. This mistakes both sides of the comparison. The most virulent enemies of the market celebrate the work of the shoemaker, cook, and hospital orderly, recognizing that they fulfill important human needs. But as the orderly, cook, and shoemaker have just such needs themselves, it is irrational to object to the observation that they make their contributions to the needs of others in a web of relations that also supply their own. The word *commodity* is meant to call to mind the idea of fungibility: bushels of wheat and, most abstractly, money. But the existence of such a web gives the coloring of human freedom and mutuality to activities and products that might otherwise be demoted to the ordinary; the market connects these contributions to the loftiest and unique. And as for money—the other aspect of markets that is supposed to make of the word *commodity* a term of abuse—the most elementary analysis shows that money is only a token for value that allows exchanges to be extended over time and space: it allows intimate connection to persons I do not know and, more wonderfully, to past and future persons. Seen in this way, money is a most marvelous (second-order) engine of human connection and interaction, hardly the "filthy lucre" of coprophilic myth.

A second, somewhat less mindless objection laments that markets replace connections of affection and generosity. But persons may be mutually generous to create value that neither alone could create. What may be called pure generosity that expects no response—not even the infant's smile of recognition, not your pleasure in hearing the opera made possible by your anonymous gift—certainly does exist, but it cannot be the ideal of human interaction, because it is either not an interaction at all or it is blind even to the reciprocal gaze of human contact.

Far more serious are the objections that accuse my analysis of fatal incoherence or of an incompleteness so radical that what I put forward as a sovereign virtue is at best a partial and perhaps subordinate aspect of human relations. Incoherence first. I prefaced this aria I sing to markets by asking you to put aside for a moment the question of what rights we have. But the question cannot be postponed indefinitely. If the rights that I enter with and that I trade on the market are not securely mine—morally secure, that is, because this is a moral argument—then this insecurity infects the rest of the argument. If I stole the thing I offer you in return for your work, I might just as well have stolen your work. I celebrate as a kind of round robin of liberty the market on which I trade with you for what a third or fourth person has made, but like an illness that plagues a large and closely interacting population, any illegitimacy in a market infects the whole. The slogan that all property is theft is an obvious exaggeration—from whom have I stolen my teeth, kidneys, and lungs?—but some property is stolen, and for my argument to go through, we had better be sure that the rights with which we enter the market and trade there are really ours.

Less dramatic, but more acute because the problem is everywhere, are the issues of the extent of our rights in time and space and along what I have called the moral dimensions. I may have a right to a piece of property, but what exactly does that entitle me to do with it, and where are the boundaries between that right and all sorts of rights you may have? You do me wrong when you take my property and you should give it back, but does this right begin to fade with the passage of time and as the property changes hands? I may have a right to move freely on the public highways, but at what speed and with what precautions?

Liberty and States

Liberty is about us as social beings, and so it is a social concept. All my examples in the first chapter were about social, political, indeed legal questions; that should not be surprising. It is not just that states are the greatest violators of liberty—they do it wholesale—but also what states are not: they are not cattle farms or mines in which inert or dumb objects, animals or rocks, are herded, extracted, cut up, or slaughtered. The state is rather nothing but a web of relations between individuals as individuals, whose choices are coordinated according to what they understand is possible for them and what they may or may not do. If law, as Lon Fuller has written, is the enterprise of subjecting human behavior to rules, then the state is the system that embodies that enterprise.[6] If states are the greatest violators of liberty, they are also its greatest enablers and protectors. In any advanced condition of civilization there can be no effective degree of liberty without the state, because there can be no effective degree of liberty without law.

You might be thinking that the threats to liberty we experience most immediately come from individuals (friends or enemies), families, employers, churches. That may be, but at least in advanced societies, behind all of these looms the state: friends and churches can only threaten our liberty if the law allows it. We may put ourselves in the hands of church officials, but that is our choice. The law may allow us to make that choice and leave us to live with its consequences, or it may limit that choice—restrict our liberty to make it—or limit the church's ability to exploit it. Throughout that range the law is the last stop, and that is why the system of laws—the state—is the ultimate system of our liberty, or of its violation.[7]

Rights

When law protects our liberty, it can be said to protect our *rights*. Anyone making a claim in terms of liberty wants some restraints imposed on others, just as he is willing to accept similar restraints. We only complain about those restraints that interfere with what we have a *right* to do, and we insist on restraints that will protect our *rights*. Rights point to those aspects of our liberty that the law—the state—should protect.

The Quebec Charter of the French Language shows how the state is implicated in the regulation of liberty (I do not yet want to say in its violation, as there is a lot more work to do before we can reach that conclusion). By regulating language, the charter, rightly or wrongly, addresses the very heart of liberty—it does (or does not) violate our rights. It does not erect something for its own sake—a building that persons who pass that way have to go around. Rather, it orders people to do something, and the order is about language. It is not even an order that stops them from saying this or that particular thing; it assumes they will go on speaking, saying all kinds of things. The charter is not about what you say but instructs you that whatever you say, you must say it in French. So it does not stop your mouth from expressing (or stuff it with) any particular thought, judgment, or order. That would certainly implicate the very heart of what it is to be an individual, whereas failing to silence a jackhammer on an adjacent construction site, which drowns out your words or makes thought impossible, would not.

The charter enters your mind in a less pointed but more pervasive way: it forces you to speak your mind—if you are to speak at all—in a particular language. It is as if you may sing any text you wish, so long as the *tune* is the one ordered by the state. When it comes to the human spirit, the music and not just the words is important. Speaking in French (not speaking in English, Yiddish, or Chinese) affirms certain social relations and cultural associations and denies others. But those social relations and cultural associations are as intimate a part of who we are, of our souls, as anything you can imagine. So I might claim that I have a *right* to speak English or Yiddish to my customers, Chinese to my patients. But what of the French-speakers? They have instituted the charter so that they may be free to speak their minds and organize their thoughts in the language of their homes and friends. They claim the right to a society where they teach their children the language they learned as children. They are afraid that they will increasingly be submerged in the English-speaking world that surrounds (and penetrates) Quebec, so that eventually they will not even want to speak French—they will have forgotten how.[8]

I can tell a similar story about the Quebec health-care system that values a certain feel to and about the health-care system, a feel of generosity, of care, of equal friendship. I am reminded of the British scholar Richard Titmuss's brief against the selling of blood.[9] Where blood is not sold, blood donation affirms and strengthens a human bond; it allows individuals to make a most personal gift to complete strangers. But where the sale of blood is allowed, there is the danger that the commercial nexus will drive out the system of free blood donation and so make impossible an act of generosity whose sincerity can hardly be matched by other acts of charity—certainly not by money contributions that may enable some to buy the blood others can only sell. (It is as if this particular language—or music—of generosity needs, like French in Quebec, to be saved from extinction.) Is it not a question, then, of liberty on both sides?

I do not need to continue the argument through the Vermont Wal-Mart example. In all of these cases, must we—the law, society, the state—not weigh the conflicting claims of right and draw their boundaries somewhere, somehow? What is left of liberty then? Does it have any force left after all these conflicts are adjudicated? Must we look to other ideas and ideals—like equality, wealth, the happiness of the majority, long life, the glory of a person, tribe, or nation, the glory of God—to draw the lines, so that in the end liberty drops out of account?

Because rights are just the boundary between an individual's liberty and the liberty of everyone else, our liberty depends on the shape of our rights. John Locke thought that a right to external possessions followed naturally from our rights to our persons:

> Every man has a property in his own person: this no body has any right to but himself. The labour of his body, and the work of his hands, we may say, are properly his. Whatsoever then he removes out of the state that nature hath provided, and left it in, he hath mixed his labour with, and joined to it something that is his own,

and thereby makes it his property. . . . For this labour being the unquestionable property of the labourer, no man but he can have a right to what that is once joined to, at least where there is enough, and as good, left in common for others.[10]

Implicit in this classic argument is the related axiom that just as I have a right over my person, so I have a right to be secure from violence against my person and the property to which my person extends. (This right is prepolitical: it is not dependent on our politics but rather judges politics. By a long tradition, such prepolitical rights are called natural rights. That is the way I use the term.) I also have a natural right not to be deprived of my liberty or my property by stealth or trickery—thus the classic argument that a man has a natural right to be secure from, and the law should secure him from, force or fraud. Finally, this rock-bottom set of natural rights entails a right freely to exchange what is mine and thus to agree to do so, from which derive the practice of promising and the law of contract.[11]

Many ask what the relevance of such arguments can be in a world in which everything is the property of somebody or of the state, so that there is certainly not "enough, and as good left in common for others."

The Shape of Rights

What the shape of our rights is—in hyperspace, as it were—has to be settled if liberty is not to be just an abstraction. This point was made wonderfully clear in an essay by Jeremy Waldron on homelessness:

Everything that is done has to be done somewhere. . . .

Some libertarians fantasize about the possibility that *all* the land in a society might be held as private property. . . . This would be catastrophic for the homeless. Since most private proprietors are already disposed to exclude him from their property, the homeless person might discover in such a libertarian paradise that there was literally *nowhere* he was allowed to be. . . . It would not be entirely mischievous to add that since, in order to exist, a person has to be *somewhere*, such a person would not be permitted to exist.[12]

Waldron goes on to make the more realistic argument that as municipalities tighten restrictions on cooking, sleeping, and urinating in public places (streets and parks), there is indeed nowhere where the homeless are allowed to do these things. The hyperspace idea is carried out in this example because a homeless person, like anyone else, has a right to be on a street or in a park, but that spatial right is limited in the dimension of what may be done there: moving, pausing, conversing with a companion, but not sleeping and perhaps not asking strangers for money.

Waldron's parable of the homeless shows how limited the rights derived from our property in our persons alone can be. My property in my person may entail an ineluctable right to see and hear, but when it comes to a right to move my legs, to lift my hands and arms, perhaps even to speak (make noise), I need space in which to do these things, and that space may not be mine. That is the point of Waldron's parable. Though I own myself, have a right over myself, I had also better have a right over at least some portion of the material world in which I move and work, if I am not to be a slave of others or of the state—even though some may say I am a part owner of the state that owns me.

It may be possible to squirm out of this very tight corner this way: I do own my energy and my intelligence. These are useful to others. Indeed, even the man who is richest in material possessions cannot get by for long without my ingenuity and effort, so he needs me, just as I need him. And even if he can bid the price for my labor way down, still at some point I have something to trade for what little he can get away with giving me.[13] At the limit, I can agree to be his slave. Indeed, Marxists would have it that all trade in goods for labor is more or less a kind of slavery. That is a particularly striking assertion, because it is the mirror image of Locke's. Locke would see the exchange of a person's labor—his property in himself—in return for goods as the quintessential exercise of liberty. The obvious synthesis of these two antitheses is some notion of rights more capacious than just a man's "property in his own person." But what could such a larger notion be? Locke would have a man's rights in his own person extend into the outside world to include all with which he "mixed his labor," but of course that generous scope for individual liberty relates to what is left out there to mix one's labor with and how the boundary is to be drawn around that part of the world that I claim to have mixed my labor with.[14]

Robert Nozick famously asked whether by pouring my can of tomato juice in the ocean I have mixed what is mine with the ocean, so as to appropriate the whole ocean, and whether by fencing a plot of land I appropriate the whole of that plot or maybe just the strip directly under the fence.[15] The argument may go on like this: even if only the minimal view is taken, no one has the right to break down my fence to get inside the perimeter I have drawn. But what if a competitor can jump or pole-vault over the fence? Without pursuing it further, this line of objection shows two deep problems about making liberty depend on rights and rights depend on my natural right to my property in my person: the problem of acquisition in a fully occupied world, and the problem of drawing the boundaries of our rights, of our possessions, even assuming we have some.

First, we are all born into a world in which very little, if anything, has no claims upon it, so that in practical effect this way of looking at it would make the extent of our liberty depend on the wildly varying accidents of our birth. Many would be limited to the right to withhold their labor and the concomitant "right" to starve. To be sure, some who are born with no claims on the outside world—it is all owned by someone else—are so shrewd, so lucky, or so talented that they can parlay the efforts that are theirs to withhold into very large pieces of the wealth the outside world holds. And if we assume some degree of holdings, some minimal level of wealth, then we can really get somewhere. With that little bit of possession, the shrewd, the inventive, or the lucky man might escalate his rights by combination and trade to quite substantial heights of accomplishment and satisfaction. And the more ordinary man may dream of this, or at least save up for a better life. The point is that if he starts out with what is *his*, then as long as he stores up, combines, and trades with others for what is *theirs*, not even the state can rightly take it away from him. (Yes, the state might wrongly take it away, but then we have left the regime of rights altogether.)

Second, we might be tempted to conclude that liberty is secure enough if we grant everyone property in—a right to—his person, which entails a right to be secure against force or fraud *and* some modest initial endowment of the physical goods in the outside world. But this way out encounters the second deep problem with the notion of rights and thus with the liberty that depends on their secure enjoyment, an objection that, if it holds good, tips us right out of liberty and into a world where the state rules and individual liberty disappears in the state's pursuit of glory, of power, or of equality. I concede that liberty of the person is empty without some modicum of right to space about the person and some initial endowment, however small, with which to begin to operate and to trade. This seemingly small concession unravels my case for liberty once we see that someone somehow must define the rights on which liberty depends. Maybe my right to my person—in Locke's sense, to my strength, my teeth, my kidneys, my mind—is a natural right: it does not depend on the state; it preexists the state and trumps its claims. But as we have seen, once a man ventures beyond his personal bubble—and even if he does not but is in the way of someone who is venturing in his— there must be a definition of rights: how far do my rights extend, when are they violated; what is the extent of my property? To all of these questions there are no natural answers. The lines must be drawn somehow, and someone must draw them. Herman Melville made that point vividly in the chapter of *Moby-Dick* called "Fast-Fish and Loose-Fish."

> After a weary and perilous chase and capture of a whale, the body may get loose from the ship by reason of a violent storm; and drifting far away to leeward, be retaken by a second whaler, who, in a calm, snugly tows it alongside, without risk of life or line. Thus the most vexatious and violent disputes would often arise between the fishermen, were there not some written or unwritten, universal, undisputed law applicable to all cases. . . .

> But though no other nation has ever had any written whaling law, yet the American fishermen have been their own legislators and lawyers in this matter. They have provided a system which for terse comprehensiveness surpasses Justinian's Pandects and the By-laws of the Chinese Society for the Suppression of Meddling with Other People's Business. Yes; these laws might be engraven on a Queen Anne's farthing, or the barb of a harpoon, and worn round the neck, so small are they.

I.   A Fast-Fish belongs to the party fast to it.

II. A Loose-Fish is fair game for anybody who can soonest
     catch it.

But what plays the mischief with this masterly code is the
admirable brevity of it, which necessitates a vast volume of com-
mentaries to expound it.

First: What is a Fast-Fish? Alive or dead a fish is technically
fast, when it is connected with an occupied ship or boat, by any
medium at all controllable by the occupant or occupants, —a
mast, an oar, a nine-inch cable, a telegraph wire, or a strand of
cobweb, it is all the same. Likewise a fish is technically fast when
it bears a waif, or any other recognised symbol of possession; so
long as the party waifing it plainly evince their [sic] ability at any
time to take it alongside, as well as their intention so to do.[16]

Property rights are inescapably conventional; at the end of the
day, the state must define or at least ratify those conventions. And
because the rights that can be claimed to be natural—that is,
established by pure reflection or wide consensus, such as our
rights to our own persons and at least to some expression—are few
and minimal, the rest must come from convention. In modern
states, that has long meant that they must be defined by law. But
liberty and rights are claims against other people and against the
state, and if it is the state that defines rights, then the argument
has moved in quite a tight circle and appears to have got nowhere.

The Myth of Ownership

In a lucid and scrupulously argued book, *The Myth of Ownership:
Taxes and Justice,* Liam Murphy and Thomas Nagel see the

answer to this one large superquestion as a matter of political morality. Their principal focus is on distributive justice: Does morality require equality, and if so, equality of what, and in what degree and kind? Is justice satisfied at the point where any greater degree of equality would decrease the well-being of all, including the worst off? Or is it sufficient if the gap between the best off and the worst off is not too great, or if the worst off are assured some measure of economic and social security? Because a world without social organization of some sort is simply unimaginable— for reasons analogous and related to the impossibility of thought without language—and social organization makes wealth possible, the question of distributive justice cannot be avoided.

Murphy and Nagel are concerned to dissolve the myth that there is such a thing as pretax ownership, so as to puncture the claim that anyone has any claims to wealth outside the tax system and before taxes are imposed. Once they have established that pretax ownership does not ground any moral claim on the design of a tax system, the way is open to resolve the question of the design by answering the question of political morality: the degrees and kinds of equality justice requires.

But taxes are not the half of it. It is not that we own only what is left after government has taken its tax bite. That bite is far bigger, because as Nozick's examples of the fence and the can of tomato juice show, everything up to the very edge of our persons is ours only by virtue of some social act of definition. So Murphy and Nagel's case of taxes is easy: pretax income is merely a bookkeeping entry on the way to after-tax income. But the inescapable conventionality of property makes even the bookkeeping entry insecure. It is not as if my acorns or bank account are mine only minus the tax levied on them. The very designation of these as mine before tax is the result of an act of social attribution.

Whether I may rightfully move down the highway on the right

or the left, at a speed greater than 40 miles per hour; whether the truck sold to me by a dealer who becomes bankrupt is mine or must be shared with his creditors; whether an ancient statue I find buried on my land or buy from a dealer is mine or belongs to the state as a national treasure; whether the right to perform a song I wrote yesterday or twenty years ago is mine or belongs to anyone who can sing it; whether my name or my picture can be used to advertise toothpaste—these are all questions that can be answered only after the law has made its definitions, its allocations. "My" song, like pretax wealth, is just a bookkeeping entry until the law has assigned it to me—or not. And this brings us back to the Montreal stonecutter. Is his liberty curtailed when he cannot lawfully carve a Hebrew inscription on his sign? Are the tools and the sign really "his," or is that just a bookkeeping preliminary to a regime that assigns them in part—in French, so to speak—to the state? Murphy and Nagel would assign to the Quebec patient his *after*-tax wealth, but I ask whether even that money is "his" in the sense that he should be free to use it to buy private insurance for private medical care. And so it is with those who would buy and sell land, build, and trade (all with *after*-tax wealth) at a Vermont Wal-Mart.

Murphy and Nagel are primarily concerned about debunking the it's-my-money objection to taxation and redistribution and thus opening the way to arguments for various measures of equality and redistribution in the design of the tax and welfare system, including variants that would make outright grants (negative taxes) to the less fortunate. But there is nothing in their arguments about the myth of ownership that limits the range of their argument to making way for the social goal of equality. If we are convinced that the highest good is the glory of a nation or of a people or of their leader, or the glory of God, or the production and maintenance of works of great beauty, then the definition and allocation of individual entitlements would all be derived from and instrumental to that good. The only supreme value that cannot easily be accommodated by this argument, that all entitlements (property) are derivative, is the supreme value of liberty. For liberty, as we have seen, depends on secure entitlements for individuals, secure against the claims of others—including that sum of all other people which is the state—whether made in the name of glory, beauty, the people's leader, or equality. And this creates a dilemma for liberal theorists such as Murphy and Nagel, committed to "the value of liberty and autonomy of the individual—freedom from interference or undue pressure in pursuing one's own course in life."[17]

I offer their arguments at some length because they are lucid, scrupulous in not overclaiming what they have and have not established, and, most important, representative of reasonable liberal thought. Here is what they say:

> The authority of the state over the individual is not unlimited. . . . Individuals . . . retain a certain degree of sovereignty over themselves, even when they are members of a collective social order. . . .
>
> The most familiar protections of this kind are the basic personal rights: freedom of expression, freedom of religion, freedom of association, privacy, and the protection of the person against physical violation. . . .
>
> Clearly, a minimal form of economic freedom is essential to a liberal system: the freedom to hold personal property with discretion to do what one wants with it. The question, though, is whether a much larger economic freedom than this—freedom to engage with minimal hindrance or conditions in significant economic activity of the sort that drives a market economy—belongs with the basic human rights as part of the authority that each of us ought to retain over our own lives. . . .

The division of opinion here is fundamental. Egalitarian liberals simply see no moral similarity between the right to speak one's mind, to practice one's religion, or to act on one's sexual inclinations, and the right to enter into a labor contract or a sale of property unencumbered by a tax bite. Denying the latter, they believe, is just not the kind of interference with autonomy that centrally threatens people's control over their lives. Some forms of personal discretion—including the basic Hegelian right to hold personal property—are at the core of the self, but unimpeded economic freedom is not one of them.[18]

Murphy and Nagel sum up the libertarian objection to their reasonable liberalism: "To champion other liberal rights while belittling economic freedom is morally inconsistent." And this is how they meet this charge of moral inconsistency:

> Conventionalism keeps being pushed aside under pressure from an unanalyzed simple intuition of what is mine and what is yours. But that intuition in fact depends on the background of a system of property law: it can't be used to evaluate the system.
>
> Evaluation must decide how "mine" and "yours" ought to be determined; it cannot start with a set of assumptions about what is mine and what is yours. The right answer will depend on what system best serves the legitimate aims of society with legitimate means and without imposing illegitimate costs. That is the only way an essentially conventional system of property, and therefore a tax scheme, can be justified.

And this "justification may refer to considerations of individual liberty . . . as well as to general welfare, equality of opportunity, and so forth. [And why may not national grandeur or the glory of the prince be included in the "so forth"?] But [the justification] cannot appeal, at the fundamental level, to property rights."[19]

But Murphy and Nagel's conception of individual liberty—even if only "the right to speak one's mind, to practice one's religion, or to act on one's sexual inclinations" or the "minimal form of economic freedom essential to a liberal system"—requires secure rights, rights against the state, rights that do not depend practically or logically on government or law.[20] Rather, government and law are bound to recognize them. What are these prepolitical rights? How can they escape the two problems I have set out in this chapter: the problem of the starting point or baseline and the problem of definition?

"Natural" Rights and the Rule of Law

Is this a way out of the dilemma that Murphy, Nagel, and all liberals of good will pose for us: we just have the rights we have (the rights the state has given us) at any particular time? This is more plausible as a resolution than at first it may seem. Recognizing the rights we have at a particular time *as rights* does give us a certain measure of security. If we know where we stand and can confidently plan our lives and arrange our relations with others starting from that secure platform, then that planning and those arrangements are at least to that extent free. Of course, if that platform is low enough—it may even be below ground—the security and "liberty" it assures mock us. Who would not rather be insecurely in possession of something than securely in possession of nothing at all? This is the abstract way of describing the choice that the abjectly poor face every day between utter destitution and precarious and fawning dependence on others—the state, family, patrons—who nonetheless provide a hand-to-mouth existence.

Alexander is said to have visited the philosopher Diogenes as he basked in his tub, to ask whether there was anything he might do for him. "Yes, I would have you step away from between me and the sun," Diogenes replied.[21] But that was in a warm climate, where perhaps grapes and olives were free for the picking. Waldron's homeless person in a completely privatized world might not be so grand. These are extreme cases, and maybe we should not build or dismantle an argument on the basis of them. (Why not?)

Is this what the idea of natural liberty is driven back to—that there is very little to which we have a natural right? Almost everything is defined by convention, that is, by the state. But liberty still may be secure if, however rights are defined at the outset, we respect each other's rights from then on and—most important—government respects them too. It is interference in the game once the rules have been set, the tokens given out, and play has begun that destroys liberty. This argument entrenches present holdings, inequalities, even deprivations against the corrective hand of government. It is *laissez-faire* married to Voltaire's Dr. Pangloss: everything is for the best in this best of all possible worlds. Why, the enemy of liberty asks, should we sanctify the result of a process, however correctly played out, if it has no moral legitimacy at the outset? Examples are everywhere. Native peoples, in America or in Australia, often live in squalor and deprivation. They are quite as free to buy and sell, work and hire, as others, but—it is said—they and their ancestors for generations have started the game with far less, because what they had was long ago taken from them by force—stolen. What kind of a story do we tell about liberty if from such a flawed beginning we come by quite regular steps to such a deplorable conclusion?

Here is a story one might tell. True, the Indians and Aborigines were horribly victimized many generations ago. So were the blacks of the Americas, who were captured like animals, sold, and brought as cargo to the continent to be slaves. But since that time, however many generations ago, they have had the same rights as anyone else, and over time the original wrong is attenuated to the point that the situation of a present-day Indian, Aborigine, or black has the same moral legitimacy as that of anyone else who (or whose parents) may have fallen on hard times, made foolish choices, or been the victim of illness and accident. Have not some blacks, Indians, Aborigines worked and traded themselves to situations far better than the average? Yes, some have, but many have not. So how can we be sure when this attenuation has erased the original wrong, or that it can ever be erased without someone's doing something about it?

There is a tough answer to this challenge. Chattel slavery and Indian dispossession were all authorized by law. And remember, we have given up on judging law, the state. All we ask is that its rules, whatever they are, be applied according to their letter. They are the rules of the game. All we can ask is that the game be played according to them, because—as we have seen—there is nothing more to ask: liberty depends on rights, rights (except maybe whatever natural rights there are) are the creatures of the state, and if whatever rights there are have been respected, then so has liberty. The blacks, Indians, and Aborigines are as free as anyone else. And there is more! If anyone now tries to take away from the better endowed to give to these others, then *that* would be theft indeed.

If that is the best we can do, then the argument for liberty is stranded on the shoals of its own relativism. No doubt a regime of regularity at least allows people to plan securely, and planning is at once an exercise of our highest rational faculties and a way of enjoying—or at least using—whatever rights we have. But this minimal view is too minimal. Some starting points can be so harsh that no amount of time can wipe out their evident injustice.

If an appeal to law without regard to the substance and source of that law were sufficient to draw the teeth of any complaint in the name of liberty, then the doctors and patients in Quebec, the Jewish stonemason, and the owners and customers of Wal-Mart Vermont would have no complaint.[22] In all those cases government was (or would be) acting strictly according to law.

Not only does the rule-of-law protection for liberty harbor the same conventionalist flaw that appears grossly and apparently in the property argument, but even its apparent if minimal advantage as a secure platform for planning is wobbly. The rule-of-law argument assumes a stable body of rules—whatever their content—that at least tell individuals what to expect and how to plan their lives against the background of this body of rules. But why do not the same considerations that justify government's *setting* the rules in the pursuit of equality, of glory, of the leader's power, not justify government's *changing* the rules when individuals' planning decisions frustrate (or even slightly hinder) those pursuits? This is most obvious with the goal of equality. However initial endowments and rules of exchange are set, whatever the tax rates and tax base, as the play goes according to them (think of a game of Monopoly or poker, where each player begins with the same stake), greater and greater inequalities may develop. Nothing, then, in the goal of equality prevents government from reshuffling the deck whenever the actual distribution moves too far from whatever the conception of equality demands. It is thought to be a virtue of the progressive income tax (with a negative tax or grant at the lower end) that it generates the desired measure of equality automatically: as people move up the income ladder, they pay a larger and larger proportion of their wealth, and they know that from the outset. But this only goes so far. Even with a progressive income tax, inequalities thought to be intolerable may be generated. And then the tax schedules would change. Only if individuals are thought to have an entitlement to the stability of rules—however much they may dislike those rules—are they secure against revisions made in the name of equality, power, or whatever.

In short, there is indeed an intimate connection between liberty and stable rules; stable rules are a necessary though not sufficient condition for a regime of liberty, but persons are entitled to that stability only in the name of liberty. The rule of law is not a value or argument distinct from and more fundamental and general than liberty. For that reason, the rule of law is not available to protect liberty against competing claims: in the end, rigorous regard for the rule of law is just an aspect of liberty, and of liberty alone. What we need is some natural—that is preconventional, deeper-than-political—account of liberty, and the rule of law will not give it to us.

But the rule of law does point the way. The reason, as we have seen, that there is an intimate connection between liberty and the rule of law is that only in a regime of secure entitlements can there be liberty. Only in such a regime are individuals able to plan and develop their lives according to their plans, secure against the imposition of others.[23] So liberty requires that we be able to plan our lives according to our judgment—that the good we pursue is the good as we see it. It is the capacity to choose and judge for ourselves that is the essence of our individuality and so of our liberty. That conclusion points to liberty of the mind as the first candidate for a natural right.

CHAPTER 4

LIBERTY OF
THE MIND

Beating and jailing political opponents, shutting down their newspapers and censoring their books, ferreting out and punishing private disloyal thoughts, are bad in every way. Condemning them tells us little about liberty, much less liberty of the mind, because such gross impositions violate the principles of democracy, of self-rule, the liberty of the ancients. Their condemnation is overdetermined. So think of this: a government regulation fixing minimum retail liquor prices. The government may think this is a way to discourage excessive drinking, or it may want to protect small retailers against competition from price-cutting chains. Whether you think this is good policy or bad, it hardly rises to the level of a violation of fundamental rights. Now what about the Rhode Island law that aimed at the same goals but left liquor prices unregulated while forbidding any advertising of those prices—not in newspapers or on television, not even in liquor store windows? All that was allowed was a small sticker on the bottle itself. The Supreme Court, which has many times permitted all kinds of price controls, balked at this law: it violates freedom of speech.[1] It was not the goal—regulating competition in liquor sales—that was the offense but the way it was done: by keeping consumers ignorant of relevant, accurate information. They literally did not know what was happening to them. Price controls reach into their pocketbooks. The advertising ban messed with their minds.

There is a critical sense in which freedom of thought is the preeminent freedom, different in kind and importance from all others. Philosophers have put this in various ways. Aristotle speaks of man as a rational animal. Kant defines human nature as free and rational. What these formulations claim is that what we desire, do, and experience is organized by our thinking. Our judgment on what comes to us by way of our senses and our choices about what we do are all backed by thinking. So even before we speak of higher modes of abstract reasoning, we must judge how to make sense of our experience and how to project our actions on the world. Freedom of the mind denies government the authority to control those judgments. Mill put it in terms of my ownership of myself—my body and my mind. How I use my body may affect others and to that extent impinge on their rights of self-ownership. How I use my mind, however, to the extent that that use affects others through *their* minds, is a matter of my own judgment and the judgment of those whom I may persuade. Perhaps my physical freedom can be restrained for the good of others or even for my own good, but government must not claim the authority to coerce what judgment I make on those restraints.

There is a political aspect to this account. Government's physical authority would be prolonged and extended if government could also control our judgment, so that, as George Orwell's *Nineteen Eighty-Four* illustrated, we ended up not only being physically controlled but liking that control. But the claim for freedom of the mind expresses a commitment more fundamental than that to democracy and self-government. The commitment is to the principle of individuality, self-ownership. It spells the limits of community and its claims. It is what is left of individualism when the force of all the arguments about our obligations to others, our dependence on others, our inevitable impact on others has been acknowledged.

The roots of this hard core of self-ownership reach into our religious past. Even in the communitarian, authoritarian tradition of the Roman Catholic Church, it has always been a premise that compelled belief is not true faith, that man can come to salvation only if he comes freely, and therefore, in the end, that a man is responsible for his own soul. This element, of course, becomes central in Protestant theology, which emphasizes each individual's personal and unmediated relationship to God. The individual's capacity and therefore right to judge both truth and goodness was a premise of the Enlightenment. So too the growth of modern science depended on the premise of the individual's ability to judge evidence and argument for himself, free from the authority—though not the argument and evidence—of tradition. The commitment to truth and reason—rationality, for short—entails a commitment to remaining open in principle to persuasion, that is, to evidence and argument. The reverse proposition also holds: rationality is in principle inconsistent with a refusal to consider arguments or evidence, that is, a refusal to allow oneself to be persuaded. Liberty of thought entails a regime in which no coercive power may legitimately limit persuasion as persuasion, because it is persuasion. Rationality is the Archimedean point—"Give me a place to stand and with a lever I can move the world"—that moves us to insist on liberty of the mind. And with that leverage, the liberty extends beyond rational persuasion to a conception of expression as broad as the concept of the mind itself.

Consider how freedom of the mind is implicated in something as benign as the Quebec language policy. Its supporters will tell you that freedom of the mind is not at all implicated: you can say or write whatever you want, including denunciations of that policy, so long as you do it in French. But that misses a crucial nuance. Our minds are not like computers encased in our skulls and running on machine code waiting to be translated into whatever application is installed and activated (though our brains may be like that). We think in language. Language, some language or other, is not only the form but the substance of our thought. (That may be the meaning of Wittgenstein's famous remark "That of which we cannot speak, thereof we must remain silent.")[2] This is the profoundest manifestation of the claim that we are social animals, that our sociability permeates or inhabits us. When we are compelled to speak in, say, French, someone is attempting to make us think in French. The attempt may fail. We may persist in thinking in English, then silently translating our English into French. That would be a subtle, perhaps undetectable act of defiance, which after a time is likely to falter. And whether or not it falters, the intent of the language law quite clearly is to get into our heads, for if thought is unavoidably thought-in-a-language, then whatever translating we may be doing, what comes out is thought in French.[3] That means that our thought as it reaches others is not quite the thought we would have chosen. It is in part dictated by others. It has to that extent been censored—words have almost literally been put in our mouths. Not only that, but who we are, how we present ourselves to others, has been censored and changed.

Is this an argument that proves too much? If we are what we

say, and if our saying must always be to an audience (even if it is an audience of persons who will read our words in another time and place), does this not contradict the very deepest premise of individuality that I have made the foundation of liberty? In the pursuit of a secure platform from which to launch my argument for liberty, I have moved all the way back to freedom of the mind. Are we confronted even there with the same difficulty that has haunted the argument all along: that all the elements with which we might want to build our argument—our property in our bodies, in what we acquire by them—have no natural boundaries, only the boundaries we construct for them as we pursue our possible goals and values (equality, power, beauty, whatever), and so cannot guide or constrain the pursuit of those values? If the very language of our thoughts is a resource constructed and shared by others, then even the claim to self-ownership of our minds is undermined.

The linguistic turn is a focused version of a claim that has received a new name and generalizing form: the social construction of reality. This is a profound challenge—profound because it implicates who we are and the nature of our reality. This challenge might be called the social construction of everything, including the social construction of the mind, and not just *the* mind but *my* mind, and not just the social construction of my mind but of *me*. Just as this social creation, the state, cannot coherently be limited by reference to rights that are its own invention, and society is fundamentally organized by entities whose reality is society's own construct, so it is with the value of physical objects and human labor, the division of the sexes and indeed the identity of the individual person, subsisting over time as the distinct and ultimate subject of discourse and attribution. But most encompassingly, it is not just social fact that is the construction of social customs, of habit, or of law but the whole of reality itself. The natural sciences are not immune but are similarly subject to subjection, as are the social sciences. Even physics and mathematics, therefore, are the constructs of our wishes.

Only in certain corners of academia are the more extreme versions of this argument taken seriously.[4] But even if the social construction of reality were a coherent position, we would still be left with the question of whether what is socially constructed is all reality, *including me*. That is, does social construction mean that my own reactions and judgments, however influenced by society, are not experienced by me as mine? This is my subjective sense of freedom, the freedom of my judgment, my responsibility for what I believe. Is that bedrock sense of my own subjectivity itself an illusion, a social construction? Some will see here a similarity to the bedrock question of freedom: whatever philosophers and scientists say about determinism and brain function, do we not have a bedrock experience of choosing, of being *free* to choose, and thus of being responsible for our choices—in fact, that our choices are indeed ours?[5] In this book on liberty I do not take on the question of freedom of the will, but my responsibility for my judgments is unavoidable. If we do not take responsibility for our own judgments, we might as well give up on thought and argument, on trying to convince others and being open to being convinced by others. As Thomas Nagel has pointed out, to argue against this is to argue nonetheless and thus to accept the premise one is arguing against.[6]

Here, then, is something that is ineluctably *mine*, however much historians, sociologists, and sociobiologists may show that it is socially constructed. To take this away from me is to rob me of my most precious possession—in other days we would have said it is to take my soul. But what would it mean to take this away from me? If this is a right that is inviolable because it is hard to imagine how anyone could violate it, no progress has been made toward a secure argument for liberty, toward an argument for a secure liberty. But of course governments violate this right regularly. That is why freedom of speech, learning, press, and association are almost invariably included at the head of the list of rights protected by liberal states. In *On Liberty*—and in Wilhelm von Humboldt's *The Limits of State Action*, on which it draws heavily—John Stuart Mill deploys his arguments and passion most convincingly, and with the fewest qualifications, to freedom of the mind. Governments violate these constitutionally protected liberties: by punishing people who say what government does not want them to say to people it does not want them to say it to—that is, if they publish or broadcast what government does not like to people whom government does not want to receive the message; by punishing people for receiving forbidden messages; or, more subtly and gently, by making it harder to send or hear certain messages just because government does not like the message.

Governments step on this liberty by controlling the behavior of either speakers (publishers, broadcasters) or their audience. Specialists in free speech theory have debated whether the ultimate interest is the speakers' or the speakers' audience's. Of course, the notion of audience must be taken broadly. Consider a form of government interference where there is no speaker or writer, as when Galileo trained his telescope on the skies and Leeuwenhoek his microscope on droplets of water. A government might very well want to stop that kind of inquiry because it might be the prelude to disturbing communications to others, or because what I learn may lead me to act in certain ways the government does not like or to be generally less amenable to follow where it would lead, or, finally, because what I find out may make me a different person from what the government would like me to be. This moves then to the situation in which a person is his own audience, as when he speaks (sings, dances) only for himself.

The government in his case too may want to control such solitary activity, as that activity may reinforce other dispositions, take time away from what the government considers worthier activity, or just contribute to making him a different kind of person from what the government would want him to be. Indeed, the two cases come close to being the same thing, as do whatever claims the government has to control these solitary activities.

In any event, the audience's interest necessarily entails the speaker's freedom: how can I have a right to hear what you have no right to say? But the speaker's freedom is not just derivative of the audience's freedom. There is no thought without expression, and expression is centrally expression to someone. It seems that even reading to oneself until quite recently was in fact reading *aloud* to oneself.[7] Uncommunicated thought may be thought indeed, and some thinkers surprise us by the revelation (communication)—sometimes posthumous—of what they have been thinking all along, but this is not only a rare but a strictly derivative phenomenon.[8] As I have argued, all thought is embodied in language—including the language of music, gesture, or image—but language came into being and exists through and for communication. And though the Quebec language law is nothing like the oppression of the Spanish Inquisition or Stalin's reign of terror, I hope it becomes clearer how offensive this seemingly mild example is.

That is the general idea, but what does freedom of the mind come to in practice? History is full of examples of government forbidding communication because it does not like what is being communicated. But that idea extends to government not only forbidding communication but also preempting it by putting words into a person's mouth—the words or the music, to accommodate the example of the Quebec language law. In the familiar and traditional example of freedom of conscience, this has taken the form of objecting not only to the prohibition of a person's chosen mode of worship but to compelled participation in "official" religious exercises. Refusing to burn a pinch of incense before the statue of the Roman emperor made many early Christians martyrs. More recently and less dramatically, the Supreme Court of the United States condemned a law requiring children to recite the pledge of allegiance to the American flag in these famous words: "If there is any fixed star in our constitutional constellation, it is that no official, high or petty, can prescribe what shall be orthodox in politics, nationalism, religion, or other matters of opinion or force citizens to confess by word or act their faith therein. If there are any circumstances which permit an exception, they do not now occur to us."[9]

These, like the oppression of totalitarian states, are relatively obvious examples. Recall that Murphy and Nagel, after arguing that our income and wealth do not belong to us until after government has decided how much we can fairly keep, nonetheless affirm that "individuals . . . retain a certain degree of sovereignty over themselves, [including] the basic personal rights: freedom of expression, freedom of religion, freedom of association, privacy, and the protection of the person against physical violation." In due course we must come also to what they refer to as the other "basic personal rights," including "a minimal form of economic freedom essential to a liberal system: the freedom to hold personal property with discretion to do what one wants with it."[10] Freedom of the mind is bedrock because it goes to the very formation of the beliefs, the desires, and the very language in terms of which we make up the "discretion" according to which one decides "what one wants." But can we have this freedom of the mind while granting that collective decisions—government—must inevitably determine the boundaries of our property and of the freedom of our persons to move about and act?

Thought and Action

Since 1872 a place has been designated in London's Hyde Park where anyone can set up a soapbox and address passersby on whatever subject and at whatever length he chooses. Hyde Park's Speaker's Corner is the very paradigm of freedom to speak (and therefore freedom to hear), the very paradigm of freedom of the mind. What if, after many complaints, letters to the *Times,* a user survey, Parliament decided that the noise and crowds around Speaker's Corner were interfering with the quiet enjoyment of the park by others, so that speech above conversational tones and gatherings of more than three persons should be forbidden? Would this be an interference with freedom of the mind? If I do not allow you to hold a political rally in my front yard, am I violating your freedom of speech? But then, are your freedom to speak and the freedom of others to hear your speech violated if the public does not allow you to speak in its front yard? Surely you are not free to hold a rally and harangue a crowd in a public library, a schoolroom, or a public hospital. Why is it so different if the public decides it wants its parks—or in any case this park—as a place of quiet and tranquillity?

Notice that the proposed ban is completely indifferent to who would speak and what they would say. Preachers, rabblerousers, lecturers on mathematics, poets, and storytellers are equally silenced. The town of Skokie, Illinois, tried to ban a march by the American Nazi Party as offensive to the town's many Jewish survivors of Nazi persecution. But imagine that the town had not allowed anyone, whether Nazis or the Veterans of Foreign Wars, to parade down Main Street during rush hour. The government would not be banning anybody's speech because it does not like what is being said, and it certainly does not put words in anybody's mouth. Is freedom of the mind therefore intact? The rabblerouser, preacher, and storyteller, the Nazis and the VFW, can choose some other public space to address the public, hire a hall, or broadcast their message by mail, by leaflet, and now on the Internet. But recall Waldron's parable of the homeless. The homeless are as free as anyone to eat, sleep, spread out and read the newspaper, and play Frisbee, except that they have no private space in which to do this, and if it is forbidden, for perfectly good reasons, in streets and parks, they have no place at all. So if you do not have access to a private hall or the Internet, and if the Hyde Park ban is extended to all parks and streets, you have no way to address your audience. And it is worse than in Waldron's case of the homeless, because streets and parks have traditionally been places to encounter one's fellow citizens. The picture is of the streets as places where everyone but the most determined recluse or the infirm must sometime or another venture to buy food, go to work, meet friends, so that the determined speaker who "stoppeth one of three, holds him with his glittering eye," and recites his tale, like Coleridge's Ancient Mariner, can find you there and try to get your attention. They are the crossroads of our common life and so the places where we may be confronted by and learn from unexpected sights, sounds, and ideas.

In American free speech law, this reality is captured in the evocatively named doctrine of the public forum. Here is the classical statement of that doctrine, from a 1939 case in which the mayor of Jersey City denied the CIO a permit to hold a public meeting on the ground that it was a communist organization:

Wherever the title of streets and parks may rest, they have immemorially been held in trust for the use of the public and, time out of mind, have been used for purposes of assembly, communicating thoughts between citizens, and discussing public questions. Such use of the streets and public places has, from ancient times, been a part of the privileges, immunities, rights, and liberties of citizens.[11]

Thus is created an irreducible space in which citizens may try to find an audience, buttonhole their fellows, speak and perhaps be heard. The streets are the indispensable place of common resort, and this doctrine reserves them as a place of individual liberty rather than pervasive public regulation.

As thrilling as this may be, it poses a difficulty for my conception of freedom of the mind. The doctrine of the public forum, the irreducible minimum space for speaking and for hearing speech, admits that the rules of property—public or private—may effectively squeeze out that freedom without government particularly trying to do that, without government in the least caring what you think, say, or hear. Your freedom of thought may be squeezed out—or at any rate squeezed down—by the same regime of property laws that shapes and, as in Waldron's example of the homeless, may squeeze down your liberty of movement and action. Or, to reverse the argument, by establishing the public forum, government enables freedom of the mind, showing that even "fundamental" individual liberty ultimately depends on public choices, choices made between competing goals, recognizing competing values—say, speech at Speaker's Corner and quiet enjoyment of the park. (There are, of course, more dramatic but less fundamental examples. Consider freedom of the mind as deployed in the political sphere in elections. After the fall of the communist regimes in the Soviet Union and eastern Europe, it was impossible without some kind of public financing to institute a regime of free elections and free press in nations where there was little private property and little discretionary income.)

A New Deal for Freedom of Speech[12]

Speaker's Corner is a very liberty-friendly tradition, as is the American doctrine of the public forum, and the instinct that has brought those societies to them is a liberty-loving instinct. But while that instinct is pragmatically satisfactory, nagging questions remain. What if, as in Waldron's thought-experiment, the public forum were to disappear? Or, more realistically, what if streets and parks are becoming obsolete as places of unavoidable public resort and universal encounter? In modern society, many citizens go directly from their garages to their cars and then to the shopping mall, or encounter each other more and more on the Internet (a largely privately owned and managed electronic network) instead of on the street.

A ready response would task the government with identifying the modern equivalents of streets and parks—whether they be shopping malls, airports, or the Internet—and forcing them open to random access in the way that serious, annoying, eccentric, and frankly deranged persons have free and random access to Speaker's Corner.[13] But once this is proposed, the cat is among the pigeons. It lays bare the fact that this fundamental liberty is one that must to some extent be designed and engineered by the state after all. And once this is conceded, then we cannot avoid the question about the criteria that will guide that engineering. Consider the national goals fostering culture, honor, and community. Should access to the Internet be guaranteed to all, or might there be some priority for "better" messages: those that are educational, improving, or of high cultural quality? Internet voluptuaries will tell you that the glory of this medium is that unlike broadcast frequencies (in the allocation of which government has made judgments of quality and social utility), capacity is effectively unlimited. There is no scarcity. Maybe, but Internet speakers must still gain access. If they want to reach a large audience, they must have access to more than just a cheap home computer, and the presentation of material more arresting than just unmediated text can require skill and resources. May the government prefer more improving messages in allocating resources and support? And what of the value of equality? May government seek to assure that all speakers have the same opportunity to reach their audience—and that all audiences have an equal opportunity to hear what is available to some?

The serious pursuit of equality would necessarily mean not just amplifying the voices of some to the volume and attractiveness of others, but turning down the volume of speakers who enjoy larger resources. The enemies of liberty have frequently pointed to this disparity as a justification for suppressing speech, lest the voices of some "drown out" those of others. Of course they do not mean that those others will literally be drowned out, but that the number and appeal (superficial and meretricious, no doubt) of competing speakers will attract more than "their fair share" of audience attention. This equalizing argument makes its most urgent appearance in proposals to limit campaign spending so that well-heeled candidates will not grab more than a "fair share" of citizens' attention. But it shows up in proposals to give more prominent television "shelf space" to educational or improving programming to counteract the proliferation of channels of communication from cable to podcast. The task, happily, is hopeless.

One solution in prosperous liberal states has been to subsidize some channels of communication—making judgments on the quality, representativeness, or worthiness of those on which public money is spent—while leaving other channels relatively unregulated and unfunded, thus open to whatever individuals choose to spend their private wealth on. Some speakers see this as a market opportunity, and they are subject to the kinds of discipline markets impose. Others may not care to make a profit but rather wish to spend their wealth, as an indulgence or as an exercise of conviction, in order to reach a general or chosen audience. That wealth may be the large aggregations that come, as in religious broadcasting, from many small collaborators—pooled either by way of investment or by members with similar convictions. Countries like the United Kingdom had government-subsidized high- and not-so-high-minded broadcast media and a free-for-all in print medium. (Compare the BBC Third Programme with the *Daily Mirror* or, in the United States, National Public Radio with the *National Inquirer*.) Indeed, newspapers, pamphlets, and books have been a sacred cow in such societies, and attempts to control or even influence what is compendiously known as "the press" have been seen as quite out of bounds. But commentators have argued that this touchiness about "freedom of the press" is at best an artifact of history and at worst a hoax played on the public by press barons, who have the most to lose by a more genuinely public-regarding regime of subsidy and control.

American law, which is the most libertarian and speech-protective of any liberal democratic regime, distinguishes between laws like those that tax the income of authors and lecturers the same as the income of professional athletes and laws specifically designed to favor some messages and disfavor others.[14] Put simply, the idea is to tolerate laws that have an incidental effect on speech and invalidate laws that try to discourage persons from conveying some particular idea. Examples are laws that require parade permits, which are designed to protect traffic and safety, and laws that allow public officials to pick and choose what groups will get such permits in terms of what cause they are marching to support, as in the case of the Nazis marching in Skokie.[15] These distinctions will sometimes be hard to make. And at the extremes certain kinds of speech—for instance, incitements to violence (shouting fire falsely in a crowded theater), publication of state secrets, pornography portraying children—will be forbidden just because of their message, but apart from these exceptions, this is the principle to which American law hews with remarkable rigor.

The upshot of this doctrine is that all kinds of messages that the community may want heard (for instance, on the health effects of tobacco or fatty fast food) will not be heard unless the state delivers them itself, and many others that collectively seem harmful (such as glamorous depictions of violence) or tawdry are in generous supply. Even benign but trivial messages may "drown out" the more valuable ones. (I will not give examples, because it is in the nature of the subject that what seems to some an obvious example of the trivial drowning out the worthwhile—say, sports broadcasting versus coverage of congressional debates—is to others an example of how the heroic and thrilling naturally attracts an audience that the boring cannot command.)

These discrepancies must not only be endured, they are thought to be the very soul of the doctrine: the economic system—including the market and the tax structure—allocates to each of us a portion of wealth (property), and then as free men and women we each use that wealth on whatever we choose, including opportunities to speak and to listen. If I am right that speech is a matter of the music as well as the words, you can see why the Quebec language law would not survive in the American constitutional regime, and so Quebec's project to protect the French language as the "music" of daily life from being drowned out by the surrounding cacophony of English would not survive.[16]

Now come critics like Owen Fiss and Cass Sunstein, who generalize Murphy and Nagel's argument that the notion of "my" pretax wealth is at worst a myth and at best a bookkeeping convenience.[17] Sunstein sees in American free speech a parallel to the moral and conceptual confusion that leads people to complain that taxes are a burden to be resented because they take "my" wealth. Our free speech regime assumes a background of general laws of property and contract that tell me what is mine and that allow me to sell, trade, or give that property away.[18] The important thing is that the government will enforce whatever arrangements I choose. If I sell my writing ability to Disney, then the government will enforce that contract, just as if I had sold Disney sandwiches to feed its employees. If I own a newspaper and contract with you to write a weekly column trumpeting my political views, you have no more right to publish articles I dislike there than you do to serve me a dinner I did not order. It is, after all, my newspaper.

The critics point out that we have long since come to accept a vast array of laws that limit my freedom to use my property as I wish and to make whatever agreements I choose, expecting the law to enforce them. Zoning laws may not only prevent me from burning tires in my front yard but demand that I paint my house a certain color or build no higher or wider than the community thinks convenient. Labor laws forbid me from contracting with my employees for them to accept less than the minimum wage, work longer than certain hours, or refrain from joining a union. A willing buyer and a willing seller risk jail if they try to pool their assets to create a monopoly. And there are whole libraries full of laws both more trivial and far more irksome than these. All these laws were resisted in their day as intolerable intrusions on liberty—the liberty peacefully to acquire property and to dispose of it as we wish. Although many such laws have been around for centuries in some limited form, in America they arrived in a spate with Franklin Roosevelt's New Deal. And the objections to them were definitively turned away. Property and contract laws, it was said, were not some neutral background regime that the state exists to honor, not tamper with. Contract and property, and the market, are no more natural and inevitable than any other contingent social arrangement. Property is regulation. With the release from the constraints of pre–New Deal magical thinking, government was set free intellectually and politically to remake society on whatever terms the public could be persuaded it wanted.

Thus is generalized the refutation of "the myth of ownership." The reallocation of income by taxes to pay for public goods and to achieve equality is not the only claim the community has on what I would like to call mine. If the state can tax my wealth in order, say, to achieve greater equality, then there is no reason that it must allow me to treat even after-tax wealth as mine for whatever purposes I choose. The Yale professors Bruce Ackerman and Ian Ayres have suggested that we might finance political campaigns in a prosperous, liberal, capitalist society by leaving everybody with the after-tax wealth the system allows them but forbidding the use of any of that wealth—what they call green dollars—to finance political activity; government would issue every citizen an equal amount of blue dollars, which could be spent only on political activity and could not be traded in for green dollars.[19] There is, of course, no end to the objections that might be raised to such a scheme, but it is easy to see what Ackerman and Ayres are getting at. They are willing—for these purposes—to tolerate the inequalities of wealth that our economic system generates but not the concomitant unequal political influence. The blue-money scheme can be seen as an extrapolation from the argument for redistributive taxation. If government can take "your" money for its purposes, it follows that government may leave some of it with you after all, but only if you spend it on certain things. If blue money, then why not yellow money, to be spent only on books, movies, and music, and only yellow to be spent on them? And if blue and yellow money, why should government not have something to say about how blue and yellow are to be spent: only on "responsible" candidates and policies; only on improving books and serious music? It is no good arguing that such specification is wrong because the money, whatever its color, is after all mine. It is no more mine than before-tax wealth.

An Argument That Proves Too Much

Here, then, is an argument that proves too much. If freedom of the mind not only depends on government but is defined by what government does, then government cannot be constrained by that freedom. Of course government and most liberal democratic regimes claim to respect that freedom to some extent or other— that is part of what earns them that designation—but that is not to say there is a fundamental right to that freedom, or that we can even know what that liberty is, apart from what government grants us. To be a fundamental right it must be a right against government, not a plea to it. So it would turn out that we have no business concluding, with Murphy and Nagel, that government must respect "the value of liberty and autonomy of the individual—freedom from interference or undue pressure in pursuing one's own course in life" or that there are "basic personal rights: freedom of expression, freedom of religion, freedom of association, privacy, and the protection of the person against physical violation."[20]

It is hard to avoid the conclusion that Sunstein's extension of the "myth of ownership" argument obliterates freedom of thought and with it all liberty—oh, not practically, for Sunstein is a decent, liberal man, but he gives liberty no grip of its own, only what the state and he in their decency will allow.

Those who leave liberty no grip try to avoid so drastic (and illiberal) a conclusion.[21] They propose that freedom of speech is an aspect and instrument of democratic self-rule. And so it is: if government may censor or manipulate what citizens say and hear about it, then their right to choose their governors can be rendered meaningless. But that is not good enough. Expression not judged to contribute to democratic deliberation enjoys no recognition—pornography, hate speech, advertising, abstract painting, music, dance, films and plays, invective, and speech demeaning other participants in the debate have all been given as examples of unprotected expression. Expressions of religious devotion may not qualify under the democratic deliberation theory, although freedom of religion is unaccountably always mentioned as a fundamental right. So if all there is to liberty of the mind is the liberty of the ancients, the liberty to reflect on, discuss, and choose one's government, it is too little.

People's lives consist of a great deal more than politics, and the subordination of the liberty of thought to political freedom is the subordination of modern liberty to politics, even if it is democratic politics. And so this most intimate of liberties would be put in the service of the state, although the state in turn is meant to be in the service of its citizens.

Without doubt, liberty of thought and expression requires some right to the resources of the world, including the space to move about and be heard, and this right must be as secure against government's competing claims as the liberty of thought itself. This concession is seized upon to justify regulating thought and expression: because speech needs material goods and material goods can be neither defined nor attributed to individuals apart from government regulation, and these definitions and attributions (as we have seen) cannot help but depend on government policies and purpose (for instance, the pursuit of equality or national power), *therefore* thought and expression too must depend on these government policies. Stanley Fish puts it bluntly in the title to his 1994 book, *There's No Such Thing as Free Speech: And It's a Good Thing Too*. But this has things backward. Material rights are distributed according to whatever criteria of fairness and community we settle on, entirely apart from a purpose to favor or hinder this or that thought. I have what income, property, and contract rights fairness dictates, and with that property I can buy whatever books, megaphones, or printing presses I can afford (alone or with others) and hire the labor of whatever persons I want to write for my newspaper or weblog. In this respect, American law has it about right. It would be unreasonable to have liberty of thought dictate all the terms of the whole regime governing property, contracts, and the like. (Indeed, it is hard to imagine just what such a total derivation would look like.) It is sufficient that whatever rules define my material rights generally and specify what agreements about these will be enforced will apply as well when I speak, listen, or think. It is sufficient that government not be allowed to gerrymander the boundaries of my material rights in order to influence what I think, say, and hear. (This is the American constitutional doctrine of content neutrality.) What, then, of poor or illiterate persons?

Poverty and illiteracy are generalized social conditions and should be addressed by government as such. The reasons poverty may be unjust have to do with much more than inability to buy books and computers or rent a speaker's platform. Advanced liberal democracies—the United States and Canada, the countries of the European Union and Japan, for instance—have gone a long way to eliminating extreme poverty and deprivation, in part at least, out of a sense that justice requires them not to leave their least fortunate citizens in that condition. Different countries in this category conceive of this obligation of justice in different ways and tolerate different degrees of disadvantage and different degrees of disparity between their less fortunate and more fortunate citizens. Let us put these differences aside for the moment and just assume that each of these countries has largely succeeded in discharging its obligation of justice—including the provision of public education—to its least advantaged citizens. Why is the regime of content neutrality then not exactly what liberty of the mind requires? The rules of property and contract, the rules defining the economic regime, do not have to be, indeed must not be, altered to operate differently where expression is at stake. Special privileges, special rules, call down special scrutiny. Subsidy invites control. If a man is free to spend his discretionary income on sporting events or opera or books, he is freer in his mind than if he has no discretionary income and he must look to the state to give him these things. Remember Ackerman and Ayres's fairy story of the different colors of money.

Dependence and Independence

To some extent I too am telling a fairy story: it is the story of prosperous citizens of prosperous nations using their varying amounts of discretionary income—what's left over after taxes, food, housing, clothing, medical care, and the like—to nourish their minds, spirits, and fancy, constrained only by the material limit of what that nourishment costs. It is a better fairy story: it celebrates the freedom of the mind rather than undermining it. What of the less prosperous citizens of the prosperous liberal democracies that are my subject? Few would deny that whatever else our society owes its citizens, it owes its children as much education as they can reasonably absorb. And what of the fact that some of the most thrilling manifestations of the life of the mind have required more than what individuals can or will provide for themselves, alone or by pooling their resources? Not only schools but universities, libraries, museums, opera companies, and symphony orchestras are everywhere supported by government to some degree as public goods.

It would be unreasonable to deny that without basic skills and fundamental knowledge, few would be capable of the calculation and judgment that enable the liberty I have been celebrating. This necessity points to a defect in my argument about the essential individuality of thought and judgment, for it concedes that the effort of others is necessary to bring the individual to the point where the mind has the capacities that support the understanding and choice that when exercised are the liberty of the mind. In this sense, the core of individual liberty depends on the support of others—just as an infant or child needs others to sustain it to the point of self-reliance. Tales, real and invented, of children abandoned in infancy and nurtured by wild animals fascinate us because—as the tongue is drawn irresistibly to a cavity—they are a sore spot in our account of ourselves: free, independent in our judgments, ultimately responsible to ourselves and yet at our beginnings utterly dependent on those who make and sustain us. In thinking of ourselves, we can take this condition of dependence as the heart of the matter and extend it to color the account of the whole of our lives and all of our capacities. Or we can acknowledge this as the analogue, at the beginning of life, to the paradox—if paradox it is—of death. Both rub our noses in our animality. And get over it: we pull ourselves up by our own metaphysical boot-straps to embrace what we in fact experience—our own freedom and rationality, dependent at either end as they may be on an animality we have not chosen. That family, friends, generous bene-factors, and recently the state have supplied the time and resources necessary to bring children past the elementary point of mental dependency can be taken to support a conception of those others as truly owning us, because they made (and make) us. Or we can thank them, pay our debt to them, and move on to emerge into liberty's broad daylight.

It is not only we who must choose between proclaiming our liberty on the one hand and making a meal of our dependence on the other. The state also has that choice. It can treat its hold on us at the beginning of our lives as a trust discharged by helping us to emerge as free and rational persons, or it can try to prolong its parental advantage by training us not for independence but for dependence and belonging. States, like parents, have done it both ways. In *On Liberty*, Mill embraced public responsibility for edu-cation and the paternalistic authority of the state to make elemen-tary education compulsory, though he most emphatically preferred that the responsibility be discharged by giving students (and their parents) subsidies to spend on whatever educational institutions might spring up to compete for their voucher dollars.

It is relatively straightforward to apply this vision to the higher forms of state intervention in the life of the mind. I have men-tioned universities, libraries, museums, cultural institutions of all sorts. Liberal states have often tried to insulate these institutions from their own grasp, choosing variants of Mill's voucher strategy or turning over the substantive choices to a wide array of inde-pendent experts, a maneuver that cannot avoid but merely postpones the question of why some should be allowed to use public money to make judgments of truth and worth for others. I will not chase that particular rabbit down its rabbit hole. There is a much more important point to be made.

A truly liberal society, if it is prosperous enough, will take care that its taxing and spending policies are sufficiently constrained that individuals are left with significant resources beyond those needed for necessities. It is this residue of discretionary income that guarantees that the state does not have the monopoly—however benevolently and expertly it exercises it—of the resources that nourish the life of the mind and spirit, the national culture. The more these resources are engrossed by the state, the less power there is to the story that the life of the mind is individual, not government property. There is, to be sure, the bedrock principle proclaimed at the beginning of this chapter: that government must not punish people who say what government does not want them to say to people it does not want them to say it to. But government does not need to use the heavy hand of prohibition and punishment; it can simply fail to support the thought it does not like. This lighter tyranny is effective only to the extent that government holds all the cards. If government is just one player among many, it is easier to see it as enlarging rather than determining choice and judgment. To the extent that my wealth is well and truly mine, to that extent the scope of my individual liberty, including the liberty of my mind, is enlarged.

Reasonable wealth and a liberal economic regime will leave enough resources in private hands to assure that individuals, alone or in groups, can thwart the ambitions of government officials bent on tyrannizing the minds of the citizens. But what of the tyranny asserted by those very groups themselves? Think of the tyranny exerted by churches and families in even those ideal states. Mill wrote about the tyranny of public opinion. How free is a person born into as benign a religious community as the Old Order Amish? They arrange everything so that the outside world does not break into their biblically ordained, simple agricultural life. Most tellingly, they will not educate their children past the completion of the eighth grade, even in defiance of local compulsory school attendance laws. The Amish accept elementary education because it prepares children "to read the Bible [and] to be good farmers and citizens," but they fear the exposure in later school years to the emphasis on "intellectual and scientific accomplishments, self-distinction, competitiveness, [and] worldly success." The Supreme Court supported this refusal of Old Order Amish to educate their children past the eighth grade as the constitutionally protected "free exercise of religion."[22] Freedom of the mind certainly includes the freedom to band together with others to create and maintain a community that thinks and lives according to the judgments of its members. But as William O. Douglas, the lone dissenting justice, saw and the Court's majority failed to see, children must be brought to a certain point of intellectual competence if the notion of free choice is to have meaning.[23] It would be Pollyannaish to argue that the system of compulsory public education has always, or even often, had that liberating effect, but at least that is its goal.

With this mistaken and sentimental enthusiasm for the picturesque ways of the Old Order Amish, contrast the wiser decisions of the Supreme Court protecting children of Jehovah's Witnesses from being compelled to recite the Pledge of Allegiance and protecting the right of parents to send their children to private schools and schools offering instruction in German, while acknowledging the authority of the state to insist on a common basic curriculum.[24] These decisions show the accommodation that a regime determined to respect the spirit of liberty will make with the hard fact that we are not born fully equipped to think and judge for ourselves. In this respect, is not Quebec rather like the Old Order Amish?

Government is not the only or even the most effective engine of tyranny over people's lives. Edmund Gosse in *Father and Son* (1907) paints a vivid and nuanced picture of his struggle to break free from parental tyranny.[25] He shows his parents as intelligent, educated, and loving. Both were devoted members of the Plymouth Brethren, an extreme evangelical sect. Gosse's mother died when he was a small boy, and his father, a distinguished Victorian naturalist, the author of several scientific works on British fauna, moved to the southwest of England with his son, where he took charge of his education. Gosse paints a picture of a strange childhood. His father would take him along on expeditions to identify and collect the small animals living in coastal tidepools. These were days of happiness and intimacy. But his father also enforced a rigorous regime of Bible study, charitable visiting, and fervent prayer. His father's hope was that Edmund would follow him as a minister to the simple rural people who made up the membership of the sect in that part of England. His reading was tightly controlled; all fiction was banned, and the work of the devil was seen everywhere. When Edmund was sent to live with a Plymouth Brethren family in London to make a start at earning a living, his father examined, hectored, and harangued him in daily letters. The young man answered these with increasing vagueness, prompting an ever more frantic inquisition, until in one extraordinary, passionate letter Gosse declared his independence from his father and his father's religion. He went on to a distinguished career as a critic, poet, and biographer, achievements for which he was knighted. One of his books is a biography of his father. (There is a fine portrait of Edmund Gosse painted in 1886 by John Singer Sargent.)

Nothing in this story seems to have anything to do with the state. Father broke no laws and did not neglect his son—on the contrary. In short, the elder Gosse gave no occasion for any but the most intrusive and tyrannical of states to intervene. Gosse's life illustrates the tyranny the family is capable of even in a generally free, indeed liberal government. Gosse did liberate himself, but at the cost of a heroic struggle. How many sons and daughters, husbands and wives—perhaps even parents—do not manage this final act of courage and so live out their lives in a condition that is not freedom at all? This too is part of the subject of liberty and shows the human contingency of the least contingent of freedoms, the freedom of the mind. I wonder whether in fact everyone does not have to engage in a struggle, not only with family but with friends, teachers, and strangers, intimidating or admired, whose acceptance seems important. Finally, there is the struggle with the inertia of one's own mind. Liberty is a matter of degree, and the mind's struggle to be free, the struggle for truth and understanding, is never complete. But the private struggle, this struggle with oneself and those closest, is different from the struggle against the chains the state would put on us. If Gosse's father had tried to maintain his authority by force, then the state would have intervened on the son's side—because Victorian England was a (relatively) liberal state.

Edmund Gosse's private struggles—all of our private struggles—take place in a context where the state will or will not support us. Gosse could declare his independence from his father; a wife can leave her tyrannical husband; we can quit our jobs or move from a gossipy village to the anonymity of the city; we can read new books and think new thoughts, and a liberal state will protect us.

But there is no escape from the state itself, except by immigration—to another state. That is what it means to define the modern state as the institution that ultimately enjoys the monopoly of force, and that is why my account of this most inward of liberties has focused on the outward chains the state would put on us.

CHAPTER 5

SEX

L'amour, tel qu'il existe dans la société, n'est que l'échange
de deux fantaisies et le contact de deux épidermes. ("Love, as
it exists in society, is nothing but the exchange of two fan-
tasies and the contact of two epidermises.")

—Nicolas de Chamfort

Sex is the most intimate of activities, rarely in any culture per-
formed in public; the activity in which the body projects
itself the shortest space beyond itself—only as far as another
body. At the same time it is fraught with social implications: it
almost always entails contact with another person, and until very
recently the continuity of society and of the human race
depended on it. Sex and the mind are alike in many ways. They

are bound up with communication; and as the mind depends on language, which in turn depends on our sociability, without sex there would be no sociability. And children and families—the sociability that comes along with sex—are the elementary units of societies. Sex and the mind are unlike in the intensity, shortness, and animality of sex. Because of society's interest in families and in its own continuity, it is no surprise that as long as there have been governments, they have been telling people with whom they may have sex, when, and how. And yet people have chafed under these controls, feeling them an offense to liberty greater perhaps even than governments' attempt to control what they think, say, and hear.

Liberty is self-ownership. Sex at least does not offer the dilemmas and uncertainties about the extent of that self-ownership examined in previous chapters—what I have called the boundary problem. If the sex is consensual, then the joining of the two personality bubbles is just about as close as you can get to the irreducible heart of self-ownership. This accounts for the strong sense that people's sex lives are their own business. The enemies of liberty are drawn to sex just because of its intimacy, its intensity, and because it seems to be so close to the baseline of self-ownership. If they can show that even there self-ownership is a myth, a mistake, a dangerous and obscuring fallacy, the removal of this cornerstone may cause the whole argument for liberty to collapse. Remember the egalitarian liberals who insist on a vast moral distance "between the right to speak one's mind, to practice one's religion, or to act on one's sexual inclinations, and the right to enter into a labor contract or a sale of property unencumbered by a tax bite."[1] Well, these egalitarians do not need to feel any embarrassment about their claim to control a man's wealth and how he acquires it if it turns out that even the right to "act on one's sexual inclinations" stands on no sound footing of self-ownership. I have hinted at how the argument against sexual liberty might go. Now let me show you just how strong it is.

Here is the plain man's sense of the thing. Sex can be so absorbing and such a powerful motivator that it can distract and detract from other interests and activities that contribute to the growth of the person and the good of society. Every parent of teenagers knows how sex can crowd out schoolwork, sports, reading, music—to the lasting loss of the child in later years. But to make this a ground for the regulation and channeling of sex is exactly to assert a social ownership of the person that reaches far deeper and more intimately than the claims of the tax collector, the occupational licensing inspector, or the zoning board. Translating society's claim to involve itself in sex into economic terms often seems slightly comical—making the profound seem banal, or the banal profound—but here it may be revealing to see sex as what economists call a leisure activity. And it is a lively debate among economists whether a person should be taxed not just on what he actually does earn but also on what he might earn if he put his talents and training to their highest and best use. Economists, who argue for a consumption tax as the soundest and most economically efficient way to extract contributions for the general good, wonder whether leisure activity (therefore sex?) should not count as a form of consumption. After all, some earn more and spend their wealth on luxury goods (so rendering themselves liable to more taxes), others spend that wealth on expensive vacations, and still others just work less and enjoy loafing (or sex).

Few liberal egalitarians or just plain egalitarians today make that argument—it smacks too much of Pol Pot—but the argument has a more general resonance as it applies to sex and the family. As sex is associated with reproduction and reproduction with the family, sex is implicated in the inequalities and injustices laid at the door of that elementary social building block. It is the physicality of reproduction and childbirth that cements the ties between parents and children. If children were allocated to couples in the way that social security numbers or postal codes are assigned, or soldiers are billeted in homes during wartime, it is unlikely that these "parents" would find it so natural to prefer their children's good to their own or to the general good. The whole idea that these are "their" children would take on a quite different and less intense coloring. And it is the strong physical tie and the fierce preferences the family creates that are among the most potent engines of inequality. Just because the family is so rooted in the physical—sex and childbirth—it has seemed to radicals of many stripes as a stumbling block to be removed from the path to a more rational social order.

To take the point further, the progression from individual to sex and from sex to family shows the indigestible nature of the starting point. It is as individuals that we are bearers of rights and have a claim to liberty—as I have said, liberty is individuality made normative. But individuality is a foundational, contingent, physical fact, even though from it arises the mind, the soul, and the abstract. Is it possible to squeeze out the contingent and physical, so that all we have left is the dimensionless point of individuality, of distinctness and separateness, from which then issue thought and choice, rationality and freedom? That may have been Kant's project in his moral theory when he sought to eliminate everything but freedom and rationality, placing all physicality in the realm of what he called heteronomy—that is, that which governs us from the outside, as contrasted to perfect autonomy.[2] The family has no place in such a radical project, but neither does sex—except as one taste, or one consumer good among many. Because such a project seems mad—mad and inhuman—reasonable, liberal-minded people like Murphy and Nagel stop far short of such a conclusion. Devoted to a conception of justice tending to the egalitarian, ordinary, reasonable people take liberty of conscience and sexual freedom to be quite different from economic liberty.

Sex and the family are a challenge not just to the egalitarian. It is no accident that the major religions have made sex one of their main concerns. Purity to the ascetic Christian or the Buddhist sage has meant keeping sex at bay. Because it so urgently proclaims our animality, it competes with, if not contradicts, the conception of the person as a temple of the deity. If the individual is the temple of the deity, then society as a whole is the city of God, which it is our duty to build. The individual is valued only as an element of this larger whole, which has the allure of beauty, of purity, or of perfect glory and power. Sex, of course, does not necessarily contradict these ideals.[3] Nor do the ideals have to be religious— except in the sense that any ideal which does not serve individuals but rather holds that individuals exist only to serve is a kind of religion. It is the physicality of sex, its momentary blotting out of everything else, that has been felt to threaten these ideals. There may also be transcendent ideals in which these very aspects of sex are celebrated as a kind of sacrament of self-forgetting, but even then the individual is more the material than the celebrant of the sacrament.

As we have seen, equality itself can be such a transcendent ideal—transcending the well-being of the individuals among whom equality is promoted. Although the equality may be the equality of individual attainment and satisfaction, it may transcend them, preferring if need be a lower level of individual satisfaction for all if only it is equal. Some feminists have urged the regulation of sex and the institution of the family, an institution that sex creates and sustains, not because of the inequalities *between* families but because of the inequalities *within* families and the inequalities between men and women, whether in families or not. Rather than focusing on class disparities, which families transmit through generations, feminists are concerned above all with the class of all women and their pervasive subordination in every aspect of life. Sex enters into this subservience of women to men as an emblem and as an engine of inequality—a subservience so pervasive that it is often invisible to both, or, if seen, is taken as natural and inevitable. Sex is an emblem of inequality because the anatomical differences between men and women assign individuals to one of the two classes, the dominant and the subordinate, and those anatomical differences are the scene and object of sex: sex desired and sex enacted. Sex is the engine of inequality because it is inflicted on women to their pain and humiliation, because the consequences of sex—pregnancy, childbirth, and parenthood—are used to make women vulnerable and to keep them subordinate as caregivers to children and servants to men. So sex is connected to family, and family is a scene and perpetuator of inequality.

To feminists who see things in this way, sex is the enemy and the regulation of sex is a weapon that the warrior of equality will deny herself only when it will not be effective. One battleground is the field of culture, in which the belief in the inevitability of sexual subordination is inculcated and perpetuated. If men and women stopped believing this, men's grip on women would loosen or would have to be maintained by brute force, which could not long prevail. That is why Catharine MacKinnon trained her sights on writings and images that show women as objects of men's sexual desire and pleasure: "Visual and verbal intrusion, access, possession, and use is predicated upon and produces physical and psychic intrusion, access, possession, and use of women by and for men for profit. . . . It is a technologically sophisticated traffic in women."[4]

Such depictions reinforce the beliefs of both men and women that women are worth less than men, that it is right for men to subordinate, use, and abuse women. The target is strategic. The law has often treated sexual depictions as offensive and demeaning in general, so that the feminists' singling out of this one subset of sex speech is not alarming. But the distaste for talking about and depicting sex at all comes from quite different sources from the regulation the feminists would impose. It is the difference between prudery and rage. (What the first of these is I will attend to later.)

Some feminists go further, much further, to conclude that sexual relations between men and women—at least in the social world as it is and is likely to continue to be —can almost never be really free, must almost always be the product and further enactment of the subordination of women.[5] What exactly should follow from this insight is not clear. At the least, these feminists would try to change the background against which men and women come together. Whether the issue is the law of the family or what counts as consent to sex, or when a sexual relation entails that a man must assume responsibility for a woman's support and well-being, the goal is always greater equality between men and women and so greater equality within the family unit, even if it means limiting the liberty of men and women to shape their relations as they think they wish.

Consider prostitution. Most societies look down on it and try to control it in one way or another. But why? A society will suppress prostitution if it has the dominant ambition to be a living representation of an ideal of purity, and sex for sale, or sex outside of certain sanctioned contexts, or sex for pleasure alone is thought to be impure. (Of course, it may tolerate prostitution in limited circumstances as the lesser of evils.) Feminists may want to suppress prostitution because they see it as a blatant assertion of men's ownership of women's bodies. Or they may think of it as a franker and therefore preferable representation of the true nature of sexual exchange than marriage, because women may get fair value for what they give up or hand over. On that view, prostitution is more like wage labor and marriage like slavery, and the two are equated only on an economic theory that sees wage labor as itself a kind of slavery and prostitution as a particularly vivid example of that slavery.[6]

Feminists would then limit the liberty of men to buy and women to sell sex depending on whether they calculated that these limitations would hinder or further the ultimate goal of a world in which the inequalities between the two have been eliminated.

But what of the intuition—very general and plausible—that just because sex is such an intimate expression of a person's liberty, that liberty is demeaned when sex is exchanged, not freely and generously, but in a crass exchange of cash? Sex is an expression, or even sacrament, of freedom, and prostitution desecrates it. Prostitution is an instance of Richard Titmuss's argument against allowing the payment of donors for blood.[7] He argues that by making blood an item of commerce, society devalues a powerful gesture of generosity and solidarity. It is as if the traffic in blood erased an especially vivid word from our common vocabulary and so diminished everyone's opportunity for expression. The parallel to sex is striking: Titmuss points out that blood freely given is less likely to be tainted; the donor is far less likely to hide abnormalities and exposure to disease.[8]

Society may want to control not only commercial sex but also sexual practices that some may think denature the act and make it an expression of brutality rather than a sign of love. And then there are sexually explicit writings and depictions, which may offend for reasons unconnected to the subordination of women. People demand that they be protected from having their noses rubbed in sex on billboards, in shop windows, in the pages of their

daily newspapers, or as they surf through the offerings on their tel-
evisions. What is called public indecency is seen as an intrusion
into privacy. People resent it not (or not necessarily) out of prud-
ishness but because they want to be able to choose the times,
places, and ways in which they are aroused: things that arouse sexually are not like texts with unwelcome or insulting arguments;
they are more like loud noises you cannot ignore, must react to.[9]

Something like this argument has been used to justify regulating not just public displays of sex but even private sexual conduct.
The idea is that, for instance, you do not actually have to witness
sex between two men to be disturbed by it. Some say—no doubt
sincerely—that they are bothered by the very thought that "it is
going on" somewhere. The philosopher Anthony Appiah has
wisely observed, "Even those who continue to think of [gay] sex
with disgust now find it harder to deny [gay] people their respect
and concern (and some of them have learned, as we all did with
our own parents, that it's better not to think too much about other
people's sex lives anyway)."[10] But some may be incapable of getting the thought out of their heads—it is like being ordered not to
think of elephants. Their claim for protection is not quite like the
claim of those who want to protect the participants in sex from having the music of love robbed of its best, most moving melodies.
Now people are not trying to protect me from myself, to protect
my capacity, but are asking for protection for themselves.

Anyone not in the grips of a theory can sympathize with this
plea, but it rests, in part at least, on a confusion. Let us grant—
though some will not grant even so much—that sexual relations
may be compatible with the liberal ideal that we must respect each
other as free and equal persons. But philosophers of freedom have
always had some difficulty capturing the richness of the ideal that
might be called sexual friendship and that many ordinary people
and much art celebrate. Kant, for instance, as a matter of justice

asked no more than a fair and free exchange of pleasure-giving, a kind of honest commercial transaction.[11] As a matter of personal morality, however, he had more trouble, because that morality insisted on not only recognizing others as free but recognizing oneself as a free and *rational* being. And that rationality causes problems, because of the very physicality of sex, the eclipse of reason in the grip of sexual passion. How can a person be said to respect himself and his own rationality if he gives himself over to an activity that blots out that rationality? The best Kant could do was to discern rationality in the connection between sex and the necessary and therefore rational activity of continuing the species.[12]

But an ideal there is, such philosophy notwithstanding. It is compounded of mutual physical satisfaction in a context of deep affection and increasing mutual trust, appreciation, and understanding. Love is the name we have for that abstract ideal of respect of the person. The very physicality, the very rational arbitrariness of sex, work into the ideal of a particularly deep knowledge of and identification with the other person. If liberty allows a person to insist on the boundaries of his self and to privilege those boundaries over the claims even of justice—that, after all, is the meaning of what liberal egalitarians like Murphy and Nagel concede to the individual—then love is the free incorporation, into that free (and, if you like, selfish) individual, of the individuality of another person. Sex can be the voluntary, fair exchange of pleasure, but that is not the ideal of love. If the claims of justice and equality stop short at the boundaries of my mind and person—self-ownership again—then love and sexual love, as I have said, can be seen as the free merging of those boundaries. That such love is associated with (but only associated with) children and family can be seen from the individual perspective as its enlargement: the love of parents for children is, ideally, not the same as the devotion of teachers, nurses, and those assigned the social task of looking out for them. It is more elemental and arbitrary, on the analogy of sexual love itself.[13]

This account of sex and love risks the ridiculous. Literature, art, music, and the experience of ordinary people, not philosophy, are the best places to look for an understanding of human love, and I do not aspire to compete with them. But it is important to offer some ideas about sex and love if I am to show how these very powerful aspects of our humanity work with and do not undermine the ideal of liberty I am developing. There is an ideal of sex and love; much sex and some love are its travesty. Many who would regulate sex—particularly in secular, liberal democracies—are moved by this ideal and are repelled by sexual expression that they think demeans it. The ideal is true and its travesties are repellent, being so bound up with the physical it seems fair to call them disgusting.[14] Yet the ideal of liberty, in which sexual love at its best is most at home, is more important still, even though some uses of that liberty may mock and denature the ideal. Liberty is the absence of imposed restraints. As individuals or as a society, we must be free to withhold our approval or even deplore sex that departs from that ideal. We must not go further, to restrain or punish it. Consider the case of truth and error. We can disagree with, refute, mock, and despise opinions that *are* wrong, but we must not forbid or punish them. To permit the degraded use of sex no more proclaims the moral equivalence of all sexual ideas and practices than allowing the publications of the flat-earth society endorses its views as valid or even plausible. As with art and thought, so with sex. The friends of liberty must be particularly astute to discern the fallacy of those who claim that what may really be falsehood, vice, and vulgarity in sexual behavior and relations are an intrusion on their liberty to pursue the ideal.

We have already encountered two arguments to watch out for: that in the world as it is today there is no such thing as voluntary sex, and that the very idea that certain "things are going on" intrudes on my privacy. Either of these could wipe out sexual liberty and confine it to the narrow limits of some ideal. This could justify the worst kind of sexual inquisition, and in the name of liberty at that! We have here a version of the boundary problem probed in earlier chapters in respect to property. Both arguments are wrong, because they evidently prove too much. They offer the sort of justifications that either have no beginning or have no end.[15]

The privacy argument first. It has no doubt become an ever more popular rhetorical move to meet an argument you cannot answer by objecting that it offends you. We are now back in the world of freedom of the mind. An argument compliments you because it assumes you can understand, reason about it, and meet it on its merits. It is mind to mind, and the "it offends me" response to an argument amounts to answering, "I am too dumb or too emotional to be able to think about what you have said." Those who are offended by "the very idea" that something they do not like is going on are not making an argument, are not reasoning with those whose liberty they would restrict. They insult not only the objects of their disgust but themselves, because they admit they cannot or will not think about, rather than just react to, what gets under their skin.[16] I hope I have made clear that I do not carry this to the point of arguing that people should have their noses rubbed in sights, sounds, and smells that offend them. To be able to walk down the street without being forced to gaze on sexually explicit posters or public displays of intimacy that go past a certain point (what point?) is certainly part of our privacy, of the courtesy we can demand of each other in the use of our common space. This also admits that explicit sex material can provoke thoughts and feelings that people may find unwelcome and should be free from. But "the very idea" is not like that. The offending actors keep to themselves; they thrust nothing on any-body. What bothers the victim of this offense comes down to the knowledge that this conduct is allowed, not punished. But as a reason for punishing something—that it is disturbing that it is not punished—the argument is almost comically circular.

That people should be protected from sexual practices because they cannot be truly voluntary—the argument some fem-inists make—is much more menacing and has a great deal more force. Certainly what looks like voluntary sex is often in fact not free at all. Drugs can cloud the mind and will so that consent means nothing. People have been tricked into agreeing to sex because they have been cheated or lied to. These are easy cases, and they are different only in degree from other actions people agree to because their reason has been clouded or they have been tricked. Threats also are an easy case. A man rapes a woman by brute force, but it is no less rape if he threatens force. And this can be generalized to any threat to do something that the rapist has no right to do—the teacher who threatens his student with a failing grade unless the student agrees to sex is a kind of rapist too.[17] But the pressure then is on what a person has a right to do. The man who offers a woman money for sex is one such case. What if a woman offers a man sex for money? Is there consent in one but not the other example—in both, or neither? Is the sex vol-untary only if both participants are moved to it by physical desire (at the same pitch)? That is a great thing when it happens, but it does not guarantee voluntary consent, nor is it obvious that it is the only motive that does. People sometimes agree to sex out of kindness, curiosity, or boredom. These nagging doubts are just a focused example of the general worry that if the situation of per-sons involved in an exchange—and sex is an exchange—is unequal, then that inequality infects the quality of the exchange.

There are two ways to respond to this concern. One is to work to remove the inequality, the other to forbid the exchange. It may be a long and hard road to remove the inequality in economic classes, or between groups (for instance, men and women, the young and the mature, the able-bodied and the handicapped), or even between individuals finding themselves in unusual, emergency situations beyond the reach of general schemes of social equality.

The road to equality is not only long and hard, but a love of liberty warns us against trying to travel to its very end. But what do we do along the way? A woman turns to prostitution as the only way to feed her children. A rich and successful model gives in to a client because she is desperately ambitious to appear in a particular magazine. Another gives in to the policeman who is about to arrest her because she is caught with cocaine. And some women become high-priced call girls when other well-paid work is available because they have a taste for luxury that they could not otherwise satisfy. Only the first of these asymmetries is systemic and demands a systemic solution: the mother's situation is proof and an example that our social system does not care as it should for mothers and their young children. That is the shame. That we allow a situation in which a mother must prostitute herself to feed her children is a crime we all commit. How does it help to make her act—or that of her customer—a crime? I am sure her customer is a bad person: if he is moved by her distress, he should relieve it, not take advantage of it. The policeman is a blackmailer: he uses a power the state has given him to extract a private benefit. Maybe the model's client is like that, at least if somebody else (the editor or designer) gave him the job of producing the best, most enticing pictures. But it may be the client's own magazine—he works for himself, and then he is like the call girl's customer. We think the sex is degraded and that both sides to the exchange mock a human ideal. But do we want to make

them criminals, to use the force of the government to stop or punish them for it? How do they harm us? There may, of course, be
the "very idea" kind of harm, but I hope that a right concern for
liberty has driven that from the field. As much as it offends us, the
"very idea" should instruct us, make us think about what good and
what denatured personal relations are like.

The communitarian theorist Michael Sandel follows a long line
of social critics who see in commercialized sex the very emblem
of a society that knows the price of everything and the value of
nothing. The call girl and the model treat as commodities what
should have an intrinsic value. The same holds true for women
who rent their bodies as surrogate mothers and citizens who sell
their votes. Some things, argue Sandel and many others, should
not be valued in money and traded in markets, formal or informal;
to do so "corrupts" them.[18] Sandel's easy examples are honorary
degrees and friendship. To be able to buy these destroys the worth
of the very good you buy. The purchased "friend" is at best an actor
who plays the role of friend—and the model or call girl might be
said to play the role of lover. So Sandel is right, but what follows
from that? Liberty teaches us that if that's what some people want
to do, we may expose and mock them. And the government does
not need to underwrite what they do by, for instance, licensing and
certifying prostitutes or even enforcing contracts for prostitution.
But liberty tells us to stop short at making them criminals.[19]

But what about baby-selling, surrogate motherhood, and vote-
buying? Surely government can make these things crimes. Yes, but
not for Sandel's reason that in all of these cases the transaction
denatures the good. Markets in babies are bad not because they
treat parents and their parenthood as commodities but because
they treat babies as commodities—and the babies don't get a say
in the transaction. Biological parents may not be the best parents,
but there are reasons (contested and contestable) having to do

with welfare of the children for making them the default guardians of the children they produce. There are fewer reasons for supposing that those who buy and sell them have the children's best interest at heart. In a sense—as with vote-buying—the sellers get money for what is not theirs to sell; they are at best trustees of it for other people's sake. I agree with Sandel that a citizen's vote is like a child: he is entrusted with it for somebody else's good or for all of our good. So vote-selling is a kind of embezzlement or breach of fiduciary duty. But it goes too far to treat sex as a trust good we embezzle when we confer it for reasons other than love or passion. If we did, then why not go on to say that my talents, my willingness to work hard, and even my blood are only entrusted to me for the common good, are not mine to sell or waste as I wish? And soon we are all, in every respect, only the state's (the government's, the community's) trustees of ourselves. And then liberty is gone.

I realize that this discussion is indeterminate, even coy, about gay sex. The spirit of liberty gags at any persecution or prosecution of adult, consensual homosexual acts. But all my talk about ideals of sexual love, of the ideal relationships of which it is a part, and of justified disgust at (unspecified) sexual practices and webs of encounter may seem like veiled references to gay sex. Kinsey estimated that as many of ten percent of males have experienced gay sex. Others have argued that bisexuality is rare and that no more than three or four percent of the population is distinctly gay in its sexual inclinations. There is also growing acceptance of the conclusion that sexual orientation is a firm, innate biological trait, though whether it is genetic or fixed during fetal development is debated. Because sex itself is a biological, not a rational, drive, it would follow that any hindrance to its expression among gay people is no more justified than it would be among those who are straight. And the relationships that gay persons form have the same potential for deepening the bonds of intimacy and love between them that heterosexual relationships do.

The difficulty is this: if gays and straights are so distinct in their sexual makeup, then the attractions and couplings of gays seem understandably strange to straights. Anthony Appiah quotes Martial's epigram *Nihil humanum mihi alienum est* ("Nothing human is foreign to me").[20] But that seems to assume a kind of omniverousness of sexual appetite that is in fact quite rare, or an effort of imagination rather like asking someone to imagine a color he has never seen. But some such effort is morally required of us if we are to respect the humanity and liberty of gay people. The alternative is to deny their humanity, which would be hideous, for we are talking of thinking, feeling human beings who are literally our brothers and sisters. That effort—and it is a possible one—is to acknowledge simply that gay people have sexual longings just like straight people do and that those longings occupy an analogous place in the geography of their spirits. That imaginative effort is, after all, perhaps only a step beyond a man's empathy for the sexual desires of a woman, and that empathy is a perfection of sexual love. To be sure, such an effort of imagination forces the straight person to abstract from the physical details of gay sex and move to a more general idea of sex. But that too reminds me of Appiah's suggestion that it may be better not to think too closely about what other people do in bed.

Punishing adult gays for the way they choose to have sex is a deep, obvious, and cruel offense against liberty—as the Supreme Court has only recently and belatedly recognized.[21] Government must stay out of their lives, and it is a mark of free societies everywhere that that is what it does. From this, what can we conclude about the vexed question of gay marriage? That, it seems to me, is a matter not of liberty but, if anything, of equality. If the government does not disadvantage gays for what they do in bed, I do not think liberty demands it to go further and celebrate it. That too is a question of liberty. One does not have to go to the wedding (or funeral) of someone whose way of life one finds distasteful (though it may show something of the liberality of one's spirit whom one treats in that way and why). Gay marriage—unlike civil unions, which allow any two persons to make legal arrangements combining their property and other material rights—is a kind of civil blessing asked of the population as a whole, and though people may (and perhaps should) be willing to give that blessing to gays as well as straights, I balk at courts forcing them to do that. That is the difference between courts in the name of liberty protecting gays from prosecution and persecution no matter what the population feels about them, and requiring this extension of the institution of marriage. That step should be taken only by people's vote, and if people vote for it, dissenters have no more right to object in the name of liberty than the courts have to impose it. This leaves many concrete issues open: Just what status does civil union create and who may enjoy it? What about adoption and other parenting relations? And finally, must we not have gay marriage after all, but as a matter not of liberty but of equality?

Recently I heard the physician, philosopher, and presidential adviser Leon Kass give a presentation about human cloning to a group of leading scientists, philosophers, law professors, and humanists.[22] He is very much against it, as are many on the commission he chairs to advise the president on this and other contentious questions, like stem-cell research. Kass has written and argued not only against human cloning but also, some years ago, against in vitro fertilization (test-tube babies). In his talk he argued against human cloning because it cuts the link between sex and reproduction. Sex is shadowed by death and by the possibility of new life. It is the dialectical synthesis between the two that solves for us—insofar as it can be solved—the problem of mortality. The child born of the sexual conjunction of pleasure and love arrives as a stranger who delights and puzzles the couple who brought her into being. She continues them in new and unexpected ways, and they love her especially for it. She is flesh of their flesh, but quite separate and different too. Cloning not only severs the connection between sex and the new child but also destroys the sense of surprise, of unexpected, unpredictable novelty. A cloned child would be a manufactured object: precisely chosen to be an exact copy of its parent. The parent would be making a belated identical twin of himself.

Kass argued from metaphor to metaphor. He was emotional and personal. He ended by reading a poem by Galway Kinnell about the inexplicably deep joy that Kinnell and his wife felt when their little boy would stumble into their room, unfailingly awakened by the sound of his parents' lovemaking, to nestle contentedly between them.[23] And Kass went so far—working the punning connection between the erotic and the etymological link between eros and striving—as to suggest that cloning puts in danger the meaning of human effort of every sort.

The audience was outraged, feeling behind these vague and poetic musings the chill breath of the Inquisition. They pointed out to Kass that he no longer carried the argument he was now making so far as to condemn in vitro fertilization. He was speechless. Others asked what his line of thought meant for adoption. Are adopted children somehow second-rate children, loved in a second-rate way by counterfeit parents? He stumbled for an answer that did not really come and when it did convinced no one. Another speaker asked if he meant that therefore gays and lesbians who one way or another considered themselves a family and had children living with them were doubly counterfeits? And finally one teacher of literature asked how all this harping on the connection between sex and reproduction worked with the fact that most people in the developed world choose to have only one or two or maybe no children. Did he really mean that with the brief exception of one or two episodes, most people's whole erotic lives—as was surely true, he said, getting visibly angry, for everyone in that room—were a kind of second-rate charade? In arguing against severing the link between reproduction and sex, Kass had also to be arguing against severing the link between sex and reproduction. Did he really mean that? Kass could not answer.

I listened with a mixture of perplexity, annoyance, embarrassment, and sneaking sympathy. I felt as if I were watching someone exhibit himself. Why was Kass's argument so deeply wrong, so squirmingly inappropriate? I think this is it: I could imagine what he was saying as part of a hushed conversation between a man and a woman considering whether to have a child in some such way. Or maybe as something a parent or close friend, maybe a priest, might say to convince an intimate not to go down this path. But here was a man who advised the president, using arguments such as these to urge legislation, the imposition of government force, the summoning up of the apparatus of police officers, prosecutors, judges, juries, and maybe prison. And I knew why we hated what this thoughtful, gentle man was saying.

CHAPTER 6

BACK TO WORK

Our liberty is sketched out by the rights we have: rights against each other, which the government must protect, and rights against the government, which it must respect. In this sense, in a modern state government is the indispensable friend of liberty and its ultimate menace. But we have been stymied by the argument that because rights are defined by the state, it makes no sense to speak of rights against the state, nor of rights that the state must protect. And if that is where things stand with rights, liberty is no better off—unless there is something wrong with the premise. If we have some rights, and therefore liberties, that are prepolitical rights which the state is bound to recognize, rights that are there before the state gets down to the business of defining rights, then, like Archimedes with his lever, we have a place to stand, and liberty can move the world. To put it in more traditional language, unless we have natural, prepolitical rights, liberty is not secure. I hope I have made the case that freedom of the mind is such a right, which the state is bound to recognize, and that the liberty of sexual expression is another. If you are persuaded that there is at least something to these claims of liberty, then we have been too quick to melt away before the argument that property rights—and economic liberty in general—are entirely the creatures of the state, so that we have only those liberties that the state defines and recognizes for its purposes (which do not, of course, include protecting liberty). After all, Murphy and Nagel concede that

> clearly, a minimal form of economic freedom is essential to a liberal system: the freedom to hold personal property with discretion to do what one wants with it. The question, though, is whether a much larger economic freedom than this—freedom to engage with minimal hindrance or conditions in significant economic activity of the sort that drives a market economy—belongs with the basic human rights as part of the authority that each of us ought to retain over our own lives.

And they suggest the connection with sex when they speak of "the right to speak one's mind, to practice one's religion, or to act on one's sexual inclinations."[1]

Here's a case: a great chess expert earns a large income by playing anyone who pays a steep fee. And here are some things the government can do about it. It can forbid playing chess altogether. It can forbid playing chess for money. It can allow playing chess for money but set the fee. It can rule that if you play for money, you must register with the government, accept a salary, and play those opponents the government assigns to you—the assignment being made for all sorts of possible reasons: it can pick the up-and-coming players who it judges will make best use of the experience, it can make the assignment a reward for some kind of service to the state, it can assign the players by lottery or pick them from a queue, it can even auction off the slots and keep the surplus. Now substitute sex for chess, and you see why granting the natural, prepolitical right to "act on one's sexual inclinations" is a concession to the idea of self-ownership that is not easily confined to the bedroom.

You might say that chess lacks the intimacy of a sexual encounter and that that makes all the difference; but on reflection, that distinction will not hold up. True, the chess game lacks the *contact de deux épidermes* Chamfort wrote of, but it is more intimate in the sense that though it is not quite an *échange de deux fantaisies*, it is a purely mental engagement, since the pieces are, after all, no more than symbols, which accomplished players can dispense with entirely. (Imagine a "professional conversationalist" who for pay will engage you in witty dialogue in units of one half-hour.) Is it the exchange of money that forfeits the players' claim to privacy, that makes their intercourse a proper subject for government regulation, that entitles the collectivity to take a cut? If so, that would mean that government can take a cut of the prostitute's earnings, or even of the nonmonetary but material tokens that lovers exchange. And of course the argument escalates past the chess players to entertainers, sports stars—as in Robert Nozick's parable about the basketball legend Wilt Chamberlain—artisans, factory workers, and those who recruit and manage them and then trade and sell their product.[2] This is the picture I have sketched of the market as the complex, extended, and ramified web of free individual exchanges. But now I hope we see better what is at stake in granting or denying that claim. If the mind, then why not sex, and if sex, then why not work? In each extension the picture is of someone venturing his person to engage with others, who will venture their persons to engage with him.

Does this take us all the way to the libertarian dream in which all state intervention in the economy, all taxation, all regulation of property is an insult to liberty on a level with thought control and invasion of the bedroom? As we have seen, the idea of property is full of trouble for the libertarian—remember Nozick's can of tomato juice poured into the ocean. In the last two chapters I have come at it from the other end: the mind and sex. The extrapolation of the argument from either end seems to prove too much. The point of talking about work is that the two lines of argument seem to collide there. Nozick writes that if we are taxed on our income at a rate of thirty-nine percent, then why are we not slaves to the state to that very extent—and of course slavery is the very type of an evil assault on liberty.[3] Where is the frontier—defined by the moral right to liberty and perhaps patrolled by constitutional courts as the guardians of our liberty—between the "minimal form of economic freedom" and "significant economic activity that the state may tax and regulate"?

The earlier discussion points to property as the more plausible marker. Waldron's example of the homeless shows that by recognizing property in one person, you limit others. Sex is different, is it not: by bestowing it on whom you wish—or on no one—you are not depriving anybody of anything, right? Well, not quite. If your body is seen as a kind of resource, then you are assigning it to one person and not another just as much as you might assign your farm or your car. Is it that your mind and your car are not that kind of property? Well, what kind is that, exactly? If we are not to abandon the idea of self-ownership entirely, must we not draw the frontier around the body and the mind, perhaps leaving external goods on the other side? But that would prove either too little or too much. It allows too little because it would give me no secure liberty to move about and so to meet the people with whom I would exchange ideas, chess moves, or sex. It proves too much because it would allow me to earn money with my mind and body—or to trade their uses for material goods—and that at once carries me beyond the envelope of the self. We need a fresh start.

Property hurts liberty by limiting the liberty of some as it establishes the liberty of others. People with little or no property are liable to suffer every kind of pain of body and mind. They are humiliated, dependent, and lack any real opportunity to enjoy the individuality of which liberty is the normative manifestation. No reader of mine will or should follow an argument that is indifferent to such suffering of his neighbor. The simplest reason, the reason that comes closest to expressing a humane intuition, is that indifference to the suffering of others tells a story about who we are, how we regard ourselves.[4] It is not just that if we easily show our backs to a neighbor in need, we can expect the same treatment if our luck turns.[5] This indifference expresses and teaches a disposition of the soul: a man's suffering does not matter; it is like the distress of the antelope caught in the jaws of a lion—"just the way things are," an event without any importance—or even like the dissolution of salt in a solvent. If that is the lesson we teach and the disposition we steel ourselves to, we do not just lose the title, we wear away the ability to feel pity, love, and human joy. All these deepest colors of our human landscape are washed out by such indifference. The Good Samaritan is not only neighbor to the man left half dead by thieves at the side of the road; he is neighbor—that is, fellow human being—to himself.

But also those rich in property cannot say that it is all due to their own effort and person alone. The claim on them is due not just to our debt to the common human resources of language and transmitted knowledge and experience; that debt is so diffuse that it makes no definite claim upon us, but rather strengthens our sense of common humanity while taming our pride in our own accomplishments. The debt is more specific and demanding than that: it is our obligation to pay our share of the common and public goods we depend on, which would vanish if no one stood ready to pay for them. These are concrete, specific goods, like courts, police, national defense, roads, and parks. There are also more general public goods, like the common benefit of an educated citizenry free of contagious or debilitating disease. Everyone is better off in a society without misery. The presence of misery in our midst erodes our sensibilities—imagine the streets of Calcutta, where men and women must wade ankle-deep, as if through a swamp of men, women, and children living without shelter, cooking, washing, and relieving themselves in the gutters, illiterate and ignorant of the basic guides to personal and social life; it also corrupts our institutions.

A society cannot prosper without stable institutions to elicit the thought and efforts of its members: stable entitlements (that is, property); regular, ready ways of engaging, transferring, and exchanging property (contracts); and transparent, dependable institutions to protect property and enforce contracts. None of this is possible without a community of trust and mutual respect. To work together, to trade, and to accept authority as an enabler rather than a hindrance to enterprise, people must trust each other, and trust requires and engenders respect. Gross inequalities are incompatible with relations of trust and respect. There can be no trust between citizens living in such radically different circumstances that they appear to inhabit different universes, to belong to different species, and not to share a common humanity—the streets of Calcutta again. By the same token, a hungry, inarticulate citizen clothed in rags is likely to receive very different treatment from a person in authority than a citizen whose status more nearly approximates (or perhaps far surpasses) that of the official. Yet it is not inequality as such that is the hindrance. If we were all equal but did not trust and respect one another, there would be neither prosperity nor happiness.[6] This hindrance is the destruction by inequality of relations of trust and respect. Justice, for instance, demands the equal treatment of all before the law. It is reasonable to expect a decently paid judge (or police officer) to be impartial between the rich and the poor, even if the first has greatly more wealth and the other has significantly less than the judge enjoys. The judicial oath requires a judge "to do equal justice to the rich and the poor"—that is, neither to bow down to one nor to condescend to the other, to be moved neither by fear or envy of the one nor by pity for the other. But it is too much to expect such impartiality when the judge regularly confronts persons so vastly worse off (or better off, for that matter) that they seem to inhabit a different affective universe from his own and each other's.

The argument has been made that all of these public goods could be dispensed with altogether, paid for on a fee basis by those who valued them, or provided by voluntary charity.[7] But that argument is radical and unconvincing—it is enough to say that such regimes have never been tried, and where they have been approximated, they have yielded societies that are inhuman and intolerable. The more puzzling point is that all of these benefits are thrust upon us. We can choose collectively which we will enjoy and at what level—and the choice must be collective—but it is not possible to live in a civilized society and turn them down completely, so we are once more in the position of arguing not about the principle but about the price, that is, the degree.

These reminders of our deep mutual dependence can be and have been used to argue that *any* work, *any* use of our liberty to produce for or satisfy ourselves is finally at the expense or sufferance of the collectivity, which can tax, regulate, or prohibit in the name of what it counts as its good. That argument covers not just the factory owner, the investor, the entrepreneur, but even the man who makes his living playing chess for a fee. You move from my chess player to one who plays before a fee-paying audience, to the impresario who arranges the match, to the property owner who rents the hall, and by very short steps you have everything.

I do not know how to tell how much we should tax wealth so that each person is paying only his fair share for the public goods he enjoys. Nor can I tell you at what point a person has so little wealth that he cannot enjoy a decent life and we are bound to help him if he cannot or will not help himself. But I know the spirit in which we determine that point and impose that tax. It is the spirit of liberty. An example of that spirit is the economist Martin Feldstein's argument that while poverty matters, inequality does not.[8] The Gini coefficient, a widely used measure of inequality in a society, plots the ratio of the incomes of the highest and lowest 10 percent of the population. In the United States, the Gini coefficient was 40.8 in 2000; in France, around 33 (1995); in the UK, around 36 (1999); in Brazil, about 59 (1998); in the Scandinavian countries, about 25 (2000); in Paraguay, almost 57 (1999); in Hong Kong, 52.5 (2001), and in the Kyrgyz Republic, 29 (2001).[9] Feldstein's point is that to worry about this ratio rather than about the actual deprivations of poverty is to disregard the well-being of persons in favor of the abstract value of income equality, so that we may be led to celebrate the economic situation in, say, the Kyrgyz Republic over that in Hong Kong or the United States, even though the worst off in the latter two places may enjoy goods and opportunities far in excess of those available to the large majority in the first. We may even ignore the possibility that the greater wealth of the top 10 percent in Hong Kong is what makes possible the better situation of the worst off there, relative to those elsewhere in China. Of course the disparity in Paraguay may be just the kind that corrupts public life and leads in that way to impositions on the poor, and in Brazil or the United States the disparity may be a measure of a society's capacity to do more for the poor. (A judge or police officer should be paid well enough that he neither resents nor is in awe of Bill Gates's billions.) But if lowering the top and so "improving" the ratio will not help the bottom (or might actually hurt them), then obsessing about the ratio announces a willingness to hurt some without helping others. Since wealth is also a rough measure of opportunity and liberty, this fixation is an explicit announcement of the priority of equality over liberty.

Focusing on the Gini coefficient as the way to fix each person's contribution to the common good would be a clear example of not setting that contribution in the spirit of liberty. Vague though that is, it is not without bite. Government must explain why it sets the level and objects of taxation as it does. What it appeals to in that explanation is the spirit in which it acts. If it taxes just to increase equality, it does not act in the spirit of liberty. If it taxes some things more than others because it judges, say, that income from playing professional sports is less worthy than income from singing grand opera, doing heart surgery, or serving in the armed forces, and it does not tax scientific prizes at all, it acts not in the spirit of liberty but in the name of beauty or national glory.

Taxation does not put the spirit of liberty to its severest test. Taxes are the price we pay for public goods. They are inescapable and, if set in the right spirit, quite consistent with liberty. But the inescapability of taxes does not make all claims to ownership a "myth." We own what we can buy with whatever income a fair and liberal system of taxation leaves in our hands. But once the tax is paid—and remember, it is assessed in order to raise the resources to supply social needs, not to privilege some forms of income over others—what we are left with is well and truly ours.

Property, its definition and regulation, is quite another matter. That is what stumped us before and drove the discussion to freedom of the mind and to sex in search of natural rights, that is, in search of the prepolitical fortresses, secure against the assaults of policy-driven definitions of property, from which the individual might with some assurance sally out into the world. The discussion of taxes suggests this picture: we have what rights we have; we use them as seems best; and to the extent that we profit by them—that is, acquire wealth in exchange for their use—we are liable to contribute to the common and public good and are entitled to keep what is left over. Being entitled to keep what is left over just means having a right to that net balance, a right whose strength derives from the rights we exercised and exchanged to get that balance in the first place.

Think of my chess player's income and what he buys with it. He must pay taxes on it like anyone else, but to take that income away because the state does not approve of his work, or thinks he would have done better to be a teacher or a nurse, is just to deny his prepolitical right to play chess with whom he wants and on what terms he wants. Now imagine that with that net income he buys a cottage on the beach on Martha's Vineyard (he is a very good chess player). His liberty is no less invaded if the state takes that cottage away or takes away only the beach rights the previous owner and all other owners enjoy. It is as if his original natural right to make a living by playing chess flowed into and energized whatever property he bought with the income he derived from that right. Now imagine further that the Commonwealth of Massachusetts wants to turn his stretch of beach into a public beach. Just to take it would be like yet another tax, but one that fell only on him, after his contribution to the common good was already fully paid up. Such an exaction has nothing to do with a person's obligation to pay his share for the privileges of a civilized society or to help relieve the distress of less fortunate fellow citizens. That is why the law of every constitutional democracy recognizes that if

the state has a particular need for a particular piece of property—
over and above its general need for resources—then it may take
that property but must pay what is called just compensation. In
other words, it may not single out particular citizens and impose
a special burden on them just because, in addition to whatever
general wealth they may have, they happen to have a particular
right, a particular item of wealth, the state needs. If it takes this
right, it must pay. That principle is set out in the Fifth Amendment to the U.S. Constitution: "nor shall private property be
taken for public use, without just compensation."

But unlike liberty of the mind and sex, property is not a natural right, or rather, there is not a natural right to any particular con-
figuration of property rights. Take my chess player's beachfront
cottage. It happens that in Massachusetts (and Maine), although
the sea is common property and no one can claim to own it, property on land extends down to the mean low-water mark at the sea's
edge.[10] But in most other states, following a rule that goes back
to Roman law, it is otherwise: private property extends no further
than the mean high-water mark.[11] The practical effect of this is
that in most states there are no private beaches, while in Massachusetts such public beaches as there are are attached to public
lands or have to be bought and paid for. Though there may be a
natural right to own property, it would be absurd to suggest that
the Massachusetts rule is a derivation of that natural right. And
so it is with the rules of property law generally. For instance, in
most places if you occupy another's land openly, without force and
without permission, for a period of years, it becomes yours, just
as if you had bought or inherited it. But no one thinks that such
a rule expresses a natural right (or violates one), and certainly not
that the period of years must be just ten, twenty, or forty.

Does this mean we can defeat my cottage-owning chess player
with the argument that if he had bought in California, he would

have had no right to keep people off "his" beach, and therefore he should not complain if Massachusetts takes his beach rights? Certainly not. Among other things, if he had bought on Point Reyes instead of Martha's Vineyard, he would have paid less, because his property would not have included a right to a private beach. But what if Massachusetts takes a different tack? Say that the legislature one day redefines private property rights so that they stop at the mean high-water mark.[12] Each rule is equally plausible, equally in accord with natural right, and after all, it is the state that defines these rules in the first place. So is this not like my earlier discussion of the rules of the road—no principle is implicated in the decision to drive on the left or the right side of the road? Well, no. First, one or another rule about beach rights was chosen originally for a reason, even though different reasons and histories moved the rules. But more crucially, what Massachusetts proposes to do to my chess-playing landowner is not like the initial choice of the rules of the road: it is more like changing from right to left in the middle of a journey and after you (and everyone else) has bought a car with the steering wheel on the left. So it is with property rules—and the whole web of laws that define our personal space, laws about what we can do, how and when and what others around us can do. Some of those rules do more than reflect an inevitable but arbitrary choice among alternatives. But even the rules-of-the-road kind of rules take root in our habits, plans, and expectations, so that changing them abruptly does violence to how we order our lives.

Let us look at both of these aspects of the web of rules that surround us—the intrinsic rightness of some for our liberty, and the importance of stability in even those that might go either way.

First, there are the rules about ourselves and our property that liberty sketches out, at least in a general way. The example of sex makes clear why liberty needs the law to protect our bodily integrity—not just to secure us from invasion by others but to give us some space to move about, to exercise our bodies. Liberty of the mind entails liberty to choose how to live our lives free from interference, except as the interference protects a like liberty for all. And these liberties of our physical persons and our minds need secure claims to some part of the external world, secure claims to property. What and how much? Again, the guide must be the spirit of liberty. Granted, the lines can be drawn many places, but those who draw them must answer the question, Why have you drawn them there?[13]

In the time of Henry III, in the thirteenth century, only the king could take "whale, sturgeon, and other royal fish."[14] He had a property interest in them, wherever they swam. Whatever the spirit that animated that line, it was surely not the spirit of liberty. Now consider a modern version: if an endangered species—say, the southwestern arroyo toad—requires a particular habitat for its survival and recovery, the person on whose land the toad is discovered may be prevented from farming, developing, or disturbing that land.[15] Is the landowner being treated like a person with a rarely beautiful voice who may be made to sing, or with a rare blood type who may be made to donate—no more than a pint every two weeks, at a time that suits him? The toad is not beautiful—it's a toad. It does not have medicinal properties, nor does it even help to keep down harmful insects. What is the spirit that moves this particular shrinking of the landowner's property rights? The imposition is not made in the name of any other person, not even persons in generations not yet born. What, then? Perhaps the claim is made in the name of the endangered species or even nature itself—whatever it would mean to speak in their name. Remember the objection of those who dislike the very idea that some people they do not know or see are having a kind of sex they find distasteful. Getting in a distant landowner's way to protect the arroyo toad looks like that: it is the very idea that a species might be disappearing that distresses those who would limit the landowner's property rights. Such a motivation offends liberty.[16]

Much more plausible are property lines drawn in the name of equality. Put aside all thought of arroyo toads and come back to the beaches of Martha's Vineyard. It is obvious how a Roman seashore property rule serves equality: there is a more equal opportunity to enjoy that marvelous amenity. The objection that everyone had an equal opportunity to buy the beach rights is true, if it is, in only the most abstract sense, which takes no account of actual people and their circumstances. The spirit of equality celebrates fraternity in the present moment, and the abstract argument looks too much like liberty all over again. Liberty competes with equality and is an engine of inequality. The spirit of equality celebrates a certain picture of all sorts of people together enjoying those beaches—much like the nature lover celebrates the survival of the arroyo toad or the undisturbed wilderness of a place so remote and inaccessible that few may ever see it, like the Arctic National Wildlife Refuge.

Liberty is not clearly set against the Roman as opposed to the Massachusetts rule of seashore property. The regime that would remove any part of nature from individual control has at least got to justify itself. (Of course, if the community buys my chess player's beach rights, that's just fine. If the price is right, then we must assume he is no worse off.) But that is not the case that stumped us—stumped us because it looked so offensive. The tough case is where the lawgiver *rewrites* the law to *switch* to a different regime. Liberty needs stability in the rules defining rights, quite apart from the actual substance of the rights, many of which in the abstract can be neither supported nor attacked in the name of liberty. A free man ventures himself in the world. Yes, there must be rules to prevent collisions, rules that tell people what is and isn't theirs to venture with. Yes, many of those rules could be one thing or another, but whatever they are, they must stay put.

Our liberty is the liberty of free and choosing men and women. It is crucial to our liberty that we should be free to be who we want to be, and that means we must be free not only in the moment but into the future. A person is not an instantaneous being existing only in and for the moment. We have a history and a prospect. How we conceive of ourselves and how others conceive of us, our ability to have friends, enemies, associates, adversaries, and lovers, demand that we have a certain steadiness of character. Otherwise, who is it that our friend enjoys and our lovers love: yesterday's man, today's, or tomorrow's? Not only projects and relations but thought itself would be impossible, for thought requires memory and consequence. An argument has steps, but they unfold in time. So does understanding. Without that continuity we might be like the protagonist in the amnesia film *Memento*, who does not know what he did yesterday or an hour ago and an hour from now will not know what he thought and did and wanted now. That would be a weird, limited, and inhuman existence.

But to exist—persist—in and through time, we not only must be disposed to plan, we must be able to plan. It is not enough for there to be rules that assign us our assets and define our space; the rules must persist through time, or else they will not enable the very exercise of liberty that made them necessary. The rules must draw lines not only in space but in time. Just as a point in space does not define a boundary but needs extension in three dimensions, so also the bounds of our liberty must have extension in the fourth dimension of time. If liberty needs this, then free men and women are entitled to it. Liberty is individuality made normative. Individuality is time-extended. This is a possible meaning for the notion that we have souls, perhaps not immortal but essentially persistent. To enable that persistence of our understanding, relations, and projects, the rules that govern us must also have persistence.

That is a very fancy and high-flown way to argue against allowing Massachusetts to deprive my chess player of his beach rights. Surely in the real world the rules that govern our lives can and do change without dissolving either our personality or our liberty.[17] Here is an example: it used to be the law that if you owned a parcel of land, you owned it in a kind of infinite cone, down to the center of the earth and up forever into the heavens. This made sense when the worry was about overhanging tree limbs (who may lop them off, who owns the fruit?) or projecting roofs or overflying partridges. But what about the jet flying over your property at thirty thousand feet? Just as total instability is inhuman, so too is complete fixity over time. One part of our freedom is the freedom to change, and as that is true of persons, so it is of the rules bounding persons. The airplane shows that. So do the computer and the Internet.[18] Our liberty to invent and to enjoy the fruits of our inventions would be destroyed if the rules of yesterday's world confined what can be done today. Thinking about airplanes, the case seems clear about the jet at thirty thousand feet, producing only a faint hum and leaving a thin, cloudlike trail of vapor: the rule must change. But what of the farmer whose field lies next to an airport, so that jets take off and land fifty feet above his house every ninety seconds?[19]

Language offers an analogy and points to an answer. Language changes, but not so fast that we cannot understand what was said last year or written a hundred years ago. Just as with the overflying airplane, language must find new words, new ways of putting them together, and if these changes have accelerated and accumulated, we may no longer understand some of what was written several hundred years ago without an effort of historical excavation. Or we may think we understand but really don't. Both

change and stability are necessary if there is to be successful communication, and communication, as we have seen, is essential to
thought. As it is with language and thought, so it is with rules and
liberty. The landowner should not feel surprised, bothered, or
cheated that now there are airlines flying overhead at thirty thousand feet. The farmer next to the airport is another matter. I shall
not work out the details here; it is enough to say that some resolutions fit more, some less with the spirit of liberty. Too many in
the wrong vein will erode our liberty.

I have said that we owe each other a debt of common humanity and we also owe the cost of public goods. And those with larger
means perhaps should pay a larger portion of those debts. I shall
not go into debates about tax rates—progressive, proportional, or
flat.[20] Some degree of progressivity I think is implicit in the purpose of easing poverty. What is quite clear is that the spirit of liberty favors taxation over regulation.[21] And if there is direct
intervention, if there is redistribution of concrete rights and goods
from a few to the many, then liberty favors taking, paying compensation, and spreading the cost to all by general taxes. Favors, but
favors only. There are plenty of cases where that would be not only
unnecessary but absurd. When Prohibition was repealed by the
Twenty-first Amendment in 1933, makers of root beer (not to
mention bootleggers) bore a disproportionate burden of the
change. Less colorfully, there are winners and losers when we shift
from a wartime to a peacetime economy, or when a high-speed
limited-access highway is built in competition with an older road
flanked by restaurants, gas stations, and motels. These are examples of lost advantages to which the beneficiaries did not have a
right in the first place. For them to complain now would be like
the man without athletic skills or striking good looks complaining
that he can't earn the salary of a professional basketball player or
movie star. I will not even sketch out when a man has that kind

of complaint, when he does or does not have a right to the advantages he enjoys. A fair system of laws, respectful of liberty, does that. It is the work of another—many other—books.[22] Rather, I return to the three examples with which I began and suggest resolutions to the puzzles they pose.

CHAPTER 7

THE SPIRIT
OF LIBERTY

I began this book with a hot-blooded declaration of love for liberty. My family saw Constant's dream of modern liberty twice turned into nightmare. Along with some carpets, dishes, and my father's talent, we moved the energy of that dream to America, where liberty is not only as real as it had been in our homeland but safe and strong. Later, as a young man thinking about liberty, I saw my students wearing Mao T-shirts and my colleagues forming Marxist reading groups and organizing to help Danny Ortega draft a constitution for Nicaragua; in 1981 I saw Hollywood, in the film *Reds*, glorifying the Lenin coup d'état that aborted Russia's parliamentary democracy. This was one long Nazi march through the Skokie of my mind. Thinking back now, I recognize the energy that brought me to law, to write about freedom of contract, to work in the Reagan administration. And in this book I decided to look at liberty, the thing itself. So, yes, I began with the Pyramids and Pol Pot, but in the end I have had to come face-to-face not with easy, fat targets but with my friends, my children, my fellow citizens of the United States and the liberal democratic world, who may not see things the way I do, who value equality and community as I love liberty, who also want to make a decent, better world. That is why I put the vivid but reasonable challenge of my three examples. That is why I hope I have put to you, my readers, the strongest, the most reasonable objections to my view of liberty. These objections have force. They move me. But liberty survives—chastened maybe, a little less fierce, a bit more . . . well, mature. And so I circle back to those first three examples to show how the ideas in the later chapters make it easier to understand why, as gentle and democratic as they may be, the impositions they exemplify are still an offense against liberty. That in turn will show what is left of my case for liberty, now that all the objections and counterarguments have been taken in and digested.

Solving the Three Puzzles

Of the three examples, the Charter of the French Language seems most offensive and illiberal. Words are put in a man's mouth, even though it is only the language, not the ideas, that is stuffed there. And benign expressions of the mind—the stonemason's sign with its Hebrew characters, the unlawfully Anglophone doll ordered by the grandmother—are suppressed with an unrelenting thoroughness. It is more than a little overwrought to recall the obliteration of all signs of Jewish breath during Hitler's campaign to make Germany and the rest of Europe *judenrein*, or the Spanish Inquisition's ferocious efforts to ferret out any remnants of the Jews and Moors expelled by Ferdinand and Isabella in 1492, its desperate drive to assure that in all places of influence there was true *limpieza de sangre*, or blood purity.[1] But as recently as 2005 there have been criminal prosecutions in Turkey of persons who carried placards using the letters *q* and *w*, forbidden because they do not appear in Atatürk's modernized alphabet.

At least no blood is shed. Neither is it by Health Canada—although surely some suffer waiting for their hip replacements, and a few may even die before their turn comes for coronary bypass surgery. As for the bargain-hunters in a Wal-Mart-less Vermont, all they lose is money. But is the impulse not the same illiberal one that puts some shared ideal ahead of the liberty and well-being of individual men and women? Perhaps those who enacted the charter thought something like this: There is a glory to the French language in Canada. It is redolent of a long and distinct past, of people, their stories, and their stubborn pride, which could not be washed away in centuries of Anglo scorn and humiliation. The use of Gaelic in Ireland and Hebrew in Israel have analogous motivations. Government rescues and protects these endangered artifacts of tribal pride in much the way it makes laws protecting the arroyo toad or a remote, unvisited wilderness, not for the benefit of anybody in particular—present or future—but just for the idea of the thing. (Sometimes the beneficiary of such individually burdensome gestures is vaguely and unhelpfully said to be mankind in general.) These are modern equivalents of the

Pyramids, raised at enormous human cost to benefit no one in particular, or like the carvings high up in the corners and under the stalls of Gothic cathedrals, where nobody can see them.[2] Here glory triumphs over the human and steps on liberty along the way.

The same analysis might underlie the Wal-Mart example. Vermont is a little like the Arctic North Slope: its rural purity must be preserved not only for the benefit of anyone in particular but also just for the idea of the thing, or for the satisfaction of knowing that it is there. Health Canada is not quite the same. Maybe some bureaucrat somewhere glories in the elegant completeness of a system that almost perfectly encloses the citizens to whom it applies. But the real point is that it installs in an urgent and intimate part of everyone's life the ideal of equality. As a monument to the ideal of equality, a total and virtually inescapable national health system bids fair to being a modern equivalent of the Great Pyramid of Giza. It elevates the ideal over the wishes and welfare of individuals just insofar as it is willing to impose equality, even if its achievement means depressing the highest, the average, or even the lowest level of satisfaction of particular persons—Pol Pot as the equality monster.

Of course, these are all quite mild impositions on liberty. Vermont shoppers can drive to New Hampshire ("Live Free or Die"), and Health Canada is not completely inescapable—you can emigrate or, if you have the savings, just go to the United States or Switzerland and pay cash for your hip replacement. And the charter by and large does not control what you say, just the language you say it in. But that is just my point. In modern, liberal, welfare-administrative democracies, the impositions on liberty are likely to be gentle, marginal. But we must be vigilant, recognize them for what they are, or we will lose our grip on what liberty is, coming to confuse it with comfort, a generalized decency, or just democracy itself—a confusion that the lovers of the state would be glad to foist upon us. But liberty is not the same as democracy. As Benjamin Constant understood, the liberty of the moderns— the liberty of individuals from the state—is far different from the liberty of the ancients, the liberty of a self-governing people.

The democracy story. There is a democracy story to be told in each of these three cases, and one in which it is the holdouts, the cranks and complainers, who offend against liberty, the liberty of the majority to define their community, their environment, their rights. Maybe decency, democracy, and equality are all there is to the story. Liberty drops out. Is it not right to see the Charter of the French Language as born of the desire of the majority of the people of Quebec to feel at home in their own country? The stonemason and his grandfather's sign with its Hebrew characters and the elderly Chinese hospital patients may not like having French words put into their mouths, but the French-speaking majority does not like having their language and the ways associated with it elbowed out of their land.

Quebec is a democracy, and are not the people of Quebec entitled to shape their environment—linguistic, cultural, as well as physical—as seems best to them? Surely if they can vote to stop factories from pumping foul gases into the air they breathe, they can try to stop their language from being overwhelmed? It is a matter of liberty both ways. Stephen Breyer, a justice of the Supreme Court of the United States, has recently argued for the priority of what he calls (citing Benjamin Constant) active liberty, the liberty of the ancients, the liberty of the people to rule themselves—and each other—by democratic processes. He writes that "active liberty helps us to preserve speech that is essential to our democratic form of government, while simultaneously permitting the law to deal effectively with such modern regulatory problems as campaign finance and product or workplace safety."[3] If campaign finance and workplace safety, why not the liberty of the people by democratic means to take control of the language of their common life? To acknowledge the stonemason's liberty—and the grandmother's in buying a doll, and the Chinese patients'—is to give those few a veto over the majority's project.

The charter forces itself into people's mouths. They can speak, write, or sing whatever they want, as long as the words are in French. But remember, language is thought—it does not just enable it—so Quebec literally dictates how I can think. True, I may think in Czech and then translate into French, but that dictates thought too, and colors its content. How does the government of Quebec know that my thoughts will lose nothing in the translation? They are mine, not the government's. And the offense will not stop at translation. It will move into what I would call first-order thought control. Because people resent what Quebec is trying to do to them, they look for ways to get around it. That is why Quebec has an Office of the French Language—the language police; think of that, a language police in a free country—to nose out violations. And nosy it is, so that an English-language newspaper was ordered to hand over photographs of a language cop photographing the English in the signs posted in the newsroom. The newspaper was accused of getting in the way of the language police doing their job. But all the newspaper was doing was showing and therefore mocking this kind of work. Punishing mockery is thought control. And that is how it often is with regulations that go against the grain. Liberty is like a stream trickling down to the sea, and regulation is like a sand dam set up to stop it. The water finds its way around the dam, so that dams must be put on either side, and then more dams around those, until the whole beach is hatch-marked with barriers.

It may be that without the pressure of the charter (and even with it), people in Quebec would more and more choose to conduct their lives in English, because that is the language of the greater world around them, or because it is cool, or because that is what more and more of the neighbors are doing. But it would be a choice. It is not that these circumstances would force them to abandon French. Many groups do hold on to languages under stress: it is a point of pride, an act of piety or defiance. Such gestures impose costs on those who make them. If everyone can be made to comply, those costs are greatly reduced. And the French in Quebec are not even a minority holding out against the larger culture; they are the majority—at least in Quebec, if not in Canada or North America or the North Atlantic community.

There may not be a finally compelling, killer argument to resolve this dispute, but the Quebec charter is not a resolution in the spirit of liberty. Why not a regime in which those who want to can speak French without paying any price other than the one implicit in seeing and hearing other people speaking to each other in different tongues? This is how it would work: Everyone would have to speak French to anyone who wants to do business in French with them. Doctors would have to treat patients who consult them in French—to refuse is to deny care to someone entitled to it. Similarly, employers must be willing to give instructions in French and merchants to receive them. Labels giving the contents of processed foods and instructions on dangerous machinery must be in French, so that the sellers' duty to warn is discharged in fact. But no one can complain if Vietnamese speak Vietnamese to each other and if Anglos put out signs in English— even whole streets of them. Does it discourage French-speakers from shopping there? So much the worse for the shopkeepers who lose that custom. And if French-speakers want to avoid merchants who will not welcome them with signs in their own language, that is a common cause the French-speakers may make; to forbid such a voluntary boycott would be as offensive as forcing the stonemason to change his sign. In the end it might not work and French might disappear from the scene, but that would be because not enough people really wanted it to be there.

Don't say, *But they did want it: they voted for it.* Voting for it is not doing it. Voting is asking government and bureaucrats and language cops to make you and everyone else do it. I can even imagine a regime that would allow a person to tie himself to the mast to avoid the siren song of English by authorizing the state to impose a language regime on *him*: a twenty-dollar fine if you catch him speaking English or going into a shop that does not advertise in French. But the Quebec charter does this to people who do not want to make such a commitment. Liberty recoils at having what goes on in my mind and comes out of my mouth determined by majority vote. It is too much like asking the state to protect me from sexual temptation by making what I might want to do a crime—a crime for everyone—so that I am protected from the very idea that it is even going on. But maybe it is more like our right not to be assaulted by sexually explicit images in shop windows, marquees, and billboards as we walk down the street: English as a kind of pornography, to be tolerated only between consenting adults behind closed doors. No. Sexy images intrude on us not only by making it harder to deny even the idea that things like that are out there; they intrude because, like loud noises or bright lights, they force themselves on our attention by going directly to our senses, without necessarily passing by way of the judging mind.[4]

Education for liberty. Granted, language goes too far. But what about schools? Liberal democratic states insist that they have both the right and the obligation to see to the education of young people from the age of five or six to about sixteen. Some of the arguments for this invoke liberty as the reason for making these early stages of education compulsory, and of course education is a direct and purposeful entry into the pupils' minds, with the unembarrassed, explicit goal of molding them. Accepting this— as most of us do—and objecting to the charter seems like swallowing a camel after meticulously straining out the odd gnat. But the argument for compulsory education is—or at least can be—a good one. It is hard because of the contingent but universal facts about what humans are. Humans are not born with, and will not of themselves acquire, the knowledge and skills necessary to the free life of the mind. In that sense we must be forced to be free. The idea—simple enough and widely believed—is that we must learn not just how to read and write but how to think clearly, to reason analytically, and that we need to master certain elementary bodies of knowledge if we are to make our way in the physical and social world. So schooling enables liberty.

At this point, if you have been taken in by the social-construction-of-everything school of thought, then you must give up on liberty, because that school of thought insists that there are no bodies of objective knowledge, no neutral techniques such as logic and mathematics, that all knowledge is ideology and all teaching indoctrination. This is an old problem and an old fallacy. But as I have said, those who argue in this way defeat themselves: after all, they do *argue* for their position.[5] The case for basic bodies of knowledge is harder, because it is undoubtedly true that what knowledge is basic depends on what kind of world we live in. A child living in an agricultural society should know more about farming, animals, and the weather than a student in the city, although both should know that the other exists, where they are, and how to get from one to the other. Not everyone must know how to repair a car or fly an airplane, but they should know that cars and planes exist.

Here again the spirit of liberty comes in. The schools can try to teach so as to allow children to grow into liberty—to show them what choices are there to be made and to give them the tools to make them. Or the schools can seize on the inevitable facts that not all alternatives can be shown, that not all claims are plausible, that even teaching mathematics and reading can move a young mind in one direction or another, and from those facts derive a license to steer pupils in a particular direction, to close off certain paths of thought (rather than just fail to point them out), to indoctrinate rather than educate for freedom. A free society and teachers who themselves love liberty will know the difference.

Of course, we are talking about compulsory education for very young children. They cannot see for themselves whether they are being taught or indoctrinated; they cannot choose—that's the whole problem. Who then can choose for them? Their parents have a certain claim; their love for their children licenses them to stand in as the proxies for their freedom in many things that the children are too young to understand and judge, from their diet and bedtime to consent to dangerous and painful surgery. Education is different from many of these, because it is about leading children to the point where they will no longer need to be led. There is no neat way out of this dilemma, but once again government can take advantage of the difficulty in order to indoctrinate children and mold them according to its own illiberal plans—just as illiberal sophists have taken advantage of the dilemma of defining property or speech rights to propose regimes that are destructive of liberty. Government can search out a solution in the spirit of liberty that looks to making children as free as possible to become themselves. As I have mentioned, John Stuart Mill proposed that the state require all young children to attend school and learn certain basic subjects, that the state subsidize those whose families could not afford to pay for such schooling, but that the state stay out of the business of supplying the schooling itself.[6] Whatever you may think of the details of this proposal, it is obviously made in the spirit of liberty. Compare it to the illiberal proposals according to which young children's schools are the places to mold their natures so that they will become enthusiastic servants of some ideal an illiberal state has chosen: its glory, equality, the service of its gods, the construction of its pyramids. This is a dilemma forced on us by the facts of our humanity—that we are born ignorant, unreasoning, and dependent. It should not be the excuse and occasion for stamping out our capacity for liberty at the very beginning. The dilemma is a challenge to the ingenuity and liberality of the liberal spirit to do the best it can.

The same dilemma and the same choices, though in a less intimate and urgent setting, come up again in the Vermont Wal-Mart example. The enemies of liberty delight in every scenario where oppression can be made to seem inevitable or, worse yet, the truest service of liberty after all—*Sicut leo rugiens circuit, quaerens quem devoret* ("The devil goes about like a roaring lion seeking whom he might devour"). It is said that the people of Vermont don't really want Wal-Marts, that they really prefer their old town centers with the friendly, familiar merchants, the slightly overpriced and distinctly tatty merchandise, and the cracker-barrel hominess of it all. And so they ask their representatives to tie them to the mast of ecological purity to protect them against their own weakness of will as they hear the siren song of consumerism.

That is a plausible but weak justification. A subtler and more persuasive explanation points to what is called the collective action problem: coercion is necessary not just to reinforce each individual's own higher purposes but to prevent cheaters, who like the feel of the old village square but try to avoid the sacrifice involved in maintaining it, from causing the practice to unravel. They are like tax evaders who actually want the benefits of government but will not pay for them if they can avoid it. In the same way, some people will be tempted to cheat and do, say, their

Christmas shopping at Wal-Mart while hoping to continue enjoying the warmth of a friendly chat in the village store as they buy
the morning newspaper or a candy bar. So we must force people
to do what they really want anyway. And how do we know they
really want it? Well, they (or their faithful representatives) voted
for it, didn't they? Voting and representative government are just
more reliable, more longheaded ways for people to choose.

In this way every imposition of government can be shown to
be the free choice of individuals. If government chooses to
aggrandize itself or to establish a green commonwealth, drastically
limiting goods and services but increasing open space and pastures
for cows, well, that's what people wanted, since they voted in the
leaders who will enact and enforce it. It is certainly true that without government, collective action problems become intractable:
taxes will not be collected, and there will be no police, no schools,
no public goods, no help for the poor, nothing that we associate
with modern life. And since these things must be chosen and their
cost allocated collectively, voting is the least bad way, the least
illiberal way, to get that done—and of course you cannot always
vote for these things issue by issue, in a plebiscitary way, but must
elect representatives and a government to choose them for you
and enforce them on you.

Anti–Wal-Martization is not quite like higher taxes for better
roads and more police. Nor is it quite like a public park or civic
monument in the town square, which some want and others do
not but all must pay for out of the town budget. Here is another
comparison: the Metropolitan Opera of New York—a national
monument—could not survive without annual public subsidies,
subsidies charged to the accounts of millions who would not
know Don Carlo from Donald Trump. If that is tolerable (and I
am not sure it is, though I love opera), then why not anti–Wal-
Martization? There is no practical way to have better roads and

more police only for those who want them. Though you can refuse to buy tickets to the opera, it's a bit much to ask you to avert your eyes as you pass the town monument paid for by public funds. The difference I sense is this: the amenity desired by people who want to shop in the village center will not survive unless they can make their crasser, consumerist neighbors shop there too.

It is this constant, active recruitment of the unwilling—as in the Charter of the French Language—this drive to close off the option of shopping elsewhere, that makes the Vermont proposal so offensive. It is as if the way we subsidized the Met were to make people spend Saturday evening there and shut down all the bars, movie houses, and bowling alleys. What the greens want is not so much open country—Wal-Mart will not encroach on much of that—but for people to live their lives in a certain way, the green way. (The charter wants you to *think* in French.) Remember that liberty prefers redistribution through graduated taxes to forced recruitment to substantive tasks. Here too, if the village center is to be a kind of bucolic theme park—a Disneyland for greens— let's tax everybody, pay the cracker-barrel merchants a subsidy to keep their stores open, and let those who want to spend what is left of their income at Wal-Mart. That doesn't sound very attractive, does it? It's not what you greens have in mind—but why not? Search your hearts: isn't it because at bottom what you want is to *make* people live the kind of life you think is best for them? That is why you are not friends of liberty.[7]

Picking your pocket. So far, in a spirit of charity, I have not mentioned another, quite plausible explanation of much legislation of the anti–Wal-Mart kind. Consider these examples: In Rhode Island, as we have seen, liquor stores were forbidden to advertise their prices, as were pharmacies in Virginia.[8] In Oklahoma and Tennessee, caskets could be sold only by licensed funeral directors.[9] Congress in 1886 put a special tax on oleomargarine colored with palm oil to look like butter.[10] In each case a benign, socially uplifting motive was offered for these burdens on liberty. Price advertising for liquor was banned to promote sobriety, and advertising for prescription drugs was banned to maintain quality in the face of competition. Funeral directors are trained to consider the feelings of the bereaved and to know the technical specifications of caskets, and colored margarine may be less healthful and fool some people into thinking that they are really buying butter.

Only lawyers would dare to offer reasons like this when any intelligent person knows that in each instance a small but politically influential group—small liquor retailers, local pharmacists, morticians, the dairy industry—have persuaded the legislature to protect them from competition at the expense of the consuming public. The liquor and pharmacy rules are very like the anti–Wal-Mart regulations, because the mom-and-pop liquor stores and pharmacies also talk about the loss of social texture when your friendly local merchants are displaced by large, impersonal, low-price chains.

Finally, consider the objections to voucher schemes like those John Stuart Mill favored. All children must attend school to bring them to a set level of proficiency. But not all must get that basic education from the state: families might be given vouchers to buy schooling from a menu of state-qualified providers. Objectors worry that society will lose a way of integrating children of diverse backgrounds into common citizenship (sound familiar?); that families peeling off from the common state school system will lose interest in making that system as good as it can be for all children (remember Health Canada). But entrenched, inefficient bureaucracies, rent-seeking custodial unions, and organizations of teachers committed to protecting seniority at all costs hate the competition and sunlight of school choice. They too pick your pocket.

These specious rationalizations mock the argument from democracy to which they shamelessly appeal. In all three of our examples there is reason to think that some such redistribution (pocket-picking) is masquerading behind the more high-minded justifications we have been looking into. But at least in the charter and Health Canada cases, it does seem that a majority benefits, and in all three we can assume that a democratic process has ratified them, and it would make my objections too easy if I systematically assumed the worst motives. But still, be suspicious—illiberal legislation may conceal a straightforward grab for power and money.

Barring the exits. Health Canada, the third puzzle, should come clearer in light of what we have seen so far. With environmentalists, it sometimes looks as if they would enlist ordinary people in the service of the idea itself—a pristine Vermont as a kind of bucolic Great Pyramid—subordinating to it such more mundane interests as a cheap Wiffle Ball set for their children at Christmas, a benign and attenuated sacrifice to a smiling green Moloch. Health Canada is about people in a way that anti–Wal-Martization may not be. Its whole energy seems directed at ministering to people when they are in situations of maximum anxiety, distress, and vulnerability. Like sex, health is very close to the intimate physical center of the individual human being. But this humane vision does not quite exhaust what determines a system like Health Canada. There is an impersonal ideal that looms over that humane impulse. It is the ideal of equality. We have seen that equality most closely mimics liberty in its concern for persons, but it peels off from that concern exactly to the extent that it can't tolerate inequality, even if those who get more take nothing from anyone else, engross no part of anyone else's portion. Indeed, a rigorous insistence on equality will not tolerate a better portion to some, even if that way the worst off are made better off.

Health Canada has some of that about it. Other nations similarly devoted to the humane ideal allow parallel private schemes, insisting only that everyone pay into the universal scheme at a level sufficient to insure a desired level for the worst off.[11] But maybe Health Canada bars the exits not in the dogged pursuit of an abstract ideal of equality but out of a realistic guess that only by keeping everyone in the same boat will there be the kind of public commitment that will enable the plan to meet the needs of the worst off. You may guess that what I say is wrong here. It is now not that the legislation sacrifices individuals to an abstract ideal of equality but that it disrespects the liberty of their minds in its drive toward its humane goal. It seems to concede that barring the exits is not a part of that goal but only a means to insure that people support it. It assumes an authority to limit the liberty of individuals and to worsen their condition, not to transfer some part of their well-being to others less fortunate but to persuade—force—them to support what their individual sound moral judgment should (Health Canada assumes) persuade them to without such pressure.

This justification for barring the exits may be seen as just another of a whole web of laws that make our choices for us, for our own good, because those making the laws think they know better than we do what is good for us. Social security is an obvious example: although it has a redistributive aspect, it is in large part a savings and insurance system, like any that might be bought from any private insurer or annuity company, with the difference that it is compulsory. It is compulsory because it is judged that many people would not transfer present income to their future selves, because they either do not have the foresight to plan for a time when they will be unable to earn or, having the foresight, lack the willpower to forgo present value for a future good. And maybe there are a few who, even looking back from misery in old age, insist they would rather have lived to the fullest when young than sacrifice anything to their later decrepitude. (*Si la jeunesse savait, si la vieillesse pouvait.*) But we may suspect that what they really think is that if they live that long and are truly miserable, family, friends, or neighbors will take pity on them and help them out.

Richard Thaler and Cass Sunstein, in examining social security and many other laws that restrict liberty for our own good, offer this further point about what are called paternalistic interventions: sometimes we must intervene in ways that at the same time offer but skew the choices proposed.[12] Salad and baked fish are good for you, and hamburgers, pizza, and rich cakes are not. Since the cafeteria in the school or the government office building or municipal arena must offer these foods in some order or other, why not in such a way that puts the bad foods last? An employer judges (quite reasonably) that it would be better for employees to put aside a certain amount of money each pay period in a tax-deferred retirement savings account. The employer does not disrespect his employees' liberty by requiring them to opt out of the plan rather than making enrollment depend on an affirmative choice to join it. There is a kind of paternalism in forcing people to make explicit choices, in confronting them with facts and alternatives they might rather ignore. But there may be no stronger natural lawlike reason for opt-in than for opt-out, for salad first than for cake and pizza first, and thus the government or employer does not act against the spirit of liberty by forcing no more than the issue.

Health Canada is not like that. It does not stop at making everybody pay, through taxes or compulsory insurance, for government-provided medical care. It bars the exits (or tries to) even for those who have paid and are now willing to pay a second time. It is the difference between paying for tuition-free state schools out of general taxes and requiring children to go only to those schools.[13] There is in these examples the added element of recruiting the personal participation and not just the money of the unwilling in order to make the scheme work. And the argument that this way we are likely to recruit not only the person but his enthusiasm, commitment, and political support just makes the offense to liberty deeper. Health Canada goes beyond giving tax-payers an interest in how their enforced contributions are spent—that incentive exists in every system funded by compulsory tax contributions: public education, social security, the British National Health—but recruits their involvement by recruiting their person.

There are justifications for Health Canada, and both of my other examples as well, that can be seen as stepping on the liberty of some only in the exercise of the liberty of others who freely (dem-ocratically) choose the good of living in a French-speaking state, of enjoying an old-fashioned village life, of having an effective health-care system for all. But in each of these the majority could get what it wants while respecting the liberty of dissenters. Not as effec-tively, you might say, but in each case I have drawn attention to the mechanism of that effect. Not only are the dissenters made to pay, but their persons are recruited and the exits are at least partially blocked even after they have paid. In that sense, their persons and not just their money are recruited. It is that extra step that gives these impositions their illiberal cast, that makes it look like the majority wants not only to achieve its ends over the dissent of the few but to make dissenters actually participate in the scheme—rather like the Romans who insisted not only that Christians obey their laws but that they burn a pinch of incense before the statues of their gods (the god of French Canadian culture, of a country unpolluted by commercialism, of equality.)

The Spirit of Liberty

Of course I have not solved the three puzzles in the sense that now any liberal-minded person must reject the Charter, or anti–Wal-Martization, or Health Canada. I have not tried to argue my case for liberty in that way, although I am a lawyer and a law professor. In court I argue to win: I want to beat the other side, be declared the winner, even have the court award costs against my opponent for having argued against me. That's how good I want my arguments to be.

In *Modern Liberty* I have put that aside. Instead I began with three gentle challenges, institutions that reasonable people might (and do) support and that yet seem in some way to trespass on our sense of liberty. In exploring that sense in the context of those three gentle challenges, I hope we have been able to get an idea of what liberty is and how it contrasts with its competitors. Liberty is the exercise of our powers as self-conscious, judging individuals, individuals who in making our own lives cannot be responsible to anyone one else except as we choose to be. And liberty is that individuality made normative. It is a refusal to be subject to anyone—even everyone—or anything, except as we choose to be.

Liberty is what defines our standing against other free people and against the government itself, which must recognize and protect that standing. That is why liberty is a relation between persons, why sickness, natural disasters, and the laws of gravity do not deprive us of our liberty. Liberty is self-ownership, and hurricanes cannot steal that from us, but other people can, although we may and sometimes should let them share it. It is also why it became necessary to establish what the boundaries between ourselves and others are. But this is where we ran into our biggest trouble. Sophists of many schools told us that there are no natural boundaries to the self, only those that society recognizes, and if that were so, there could be no boundaries against society at all. That is what drove the discussion back to freedom of the mind and the natural boundary that freedom describes, and from that to the natural boundary about our most intimate person.

Even as I tried to convince you that you do not want to deny self-ownership in the mind and the intimate body, it was obvious that I could not compel you to my way of thinking. Both in form and substance I have tried only to have "the forceless force of the better argument work its gentle effect."[14] And so I have painted my arguments with a brush, not forced them on you with a shil-lelagh. I have tried as often as I could to imagine what the best argument against what I say is and then leave it to you to choose. In this I have been guided by the words and example of my fellow friend of liberty, Bob Nozick:

> At no point is the [reader] forced to accept anything. He moves along gently, exploring his own and the author's thoughts. . . .
>
> With this manner of writing, an author might circle back more than once to the same topic. Not everything can be said at once or twice; a reader may not be ready yet to think it all himself.[15]

I speak of freedom of the mind, but I have nothing to say about whether it extends so far as to protect libels and insults, incite-ments to violence—all the ins and outs of First Amendment jurisprudence that are grist for the lawyer's mill.[16] There is a chap-ter on sex and liberty but not one word about abortion. I speak of property and work but have little to say about the details of how concrete political regimes might strike a balance between individ-ual liberty and the wishes of a ruling party—perhaps representing a majority—to further that party's own concerted interests or perhaps to realize some abstract ideal like equality or the glory of the nation.

That a majority party should be able to realize its goals is a tenet of democracy. That it should be constrained in that pursuit by respect for individual rights—liberty—is a function of liberal constitutionalism. Different liberal constitutional regimes strike the balance at different places, but all respect not only political but personal liberties, and personal liberties not only of thought, conscience, and intimate association but of work and property too. For instance, "careers open to talent" is a slogan that goes back to Enlightenment times,[17] and no taking of property for public use without compensation to the owner is a constitutional principle echoed in norms of international law.[18] But there are intricate lines to be drawn, for instance, between respect for the principle of free choice of professions and the reasonable demand that doctors, pharmacists, lawyers, accountants, and many others be competent and that the government certify that competence. Sometimes those lines are drawn in ways that suggest that government certification has fallen into the hands of a clique which is simply trying to protect its monopoly against competitors that would drive down its prices or expose its inadequacies. Nowhere is the bad-faith invocation of this benign purpose of protecting the public against incompetence more evident than in regimes that would license and certify journalists or even authors and publishers in general.[19] Similarly, there are difficult lines to be drawn between the definition and regulation of property and its frank expropriation. To rule that a person keeps his land but may use it only as a public park is to take that land, but short of that there are many nuanced gradations.[20] It would need a legal treatise to mark out these many distinctions, and even that could not claim that the lines it draws are somehow rigorously and uniquely entailed by the principle of liberty.

That is why I have not really *solved* the three puzzles I began with. In each case a modern, complex government will have to draw lines adjudicating between competing interests: the liberty interests of individuals competing with the liberty interests of the collective majority (the liberty of the ancients, Breyer's "active liberty").

Each of the three examples offered similar difficulties, and all I could do was bring to the surface the deep commitments that may undergird the particular solutions that were chosen. The conflict between those commitments—to tradition and group identity, to natural beauty and a particular kind of physical environment, to social solidarity and humane treatment of all suffering people—and individual liberty cannot be definitively resolved by any formula or deduction from first principles. General principles can carry us only so far: they are like an architect's drawings for an elegant skyscraper. They give you a sense of what the building will look like but do not work out the details of the plumbing, basement, subbasements, and mechanicals. These details are what constitutions, laws, traditions, and practices supply.[21] They lack the grandeur of the vision for the tower, but they are indispensable if the building is ever to be built and, when built, if it is to stand up and work. Lawyers, judges, legislators, and economists are the engineers who will work out these unglamorous details. And when the building is built, they will work in the basement as the plumbers and handymen of liberty. That is where I work when I am not writing books like this. We are all architects, and the buildings we design will—I hope—all look different. What this book has tried to show is what a building built in the spirit of liberty might look like, but I have not taken you into the basement and subbasements more than I have had to. It is up to you to see if we all, the architects, have built in the spirit of liberty and the maintenance crew have kept it in that spirit.

NOTES

CHAPTER 1.
LIBERTY: THE VERY IDEA

Epigraphs: Yeats quoted in R. F. Foster, *W. B. Yeats: A Life* (New York: Oxford University Press, 2003), p. 265. Benjamin Constant, "De la liberté des anciens comparée à celle des modernes," lecture delivered at the Athénée Royal de Paris, 1819, available at www.panarchy.org/constant/liberte.1819.html. The translation is mine, as are all others.

1. Constant, "De la liberté." For a different view of Constant's work, see Stephen Breyer, *Active Liberty: Interpreting Our Democratic Constitution* (New York: Knopf, 2005). Given Constant's personality, it is not surprising that his words have been susceptible to varying interpretations.

    Constant was hardly a model of resolution, rectitude, or consistency, in either his political alliances or his tempestuous love life. He despised the ancien régime but deplored as well the excesses of the Jacobins, supporting the government that followed. He opposed Napoleon and left France to avoid Napoleon's secret police, returned to France in hopes of supporting a constitutional monarchy, rallied to Napoleon on his return from Elba, but then rallied to the support (or at least the patronage) of the restored Bourbon monarchy, under which he attained office and support. This may explain why at the end of his *discours* to his audience at the Royal Atheneum, he pulls in his horns: "Far, gentlemen, from renouncing either of the two forms of liberty, one must, I have shown, learn to combine the two." *Sola Inconstantia Constans* was the device he had chosen for himself. His friend and sometime mistress, Madame de Staël, was a more courageous and admirable character. She put herself at risk sheltering émigrés during the terror and traveled to Russia and Sweden to encourage support against Napoleon. My principal source for details of Constant's life is Dennis Wood, *Benjamin Constant: A Biography* (New York: Routledge 1993); see also Harold Nicolson, *Benjamin Constant* (London: Constable, 1949).

2. Émile Faguet, "Benjamin Constant," in *Politiques et Moralistes du Dix-Neuvième Siècle* (1st ed.), available at fare.tunes.org/books/Faguet/benjamin_constant.html. The translation is mine.

3. Isaiah Berlin, "Two Concepts of Liberty," in *Four Essays on Liberty* (Oxford: Oxford University Press, 1969), pp. xlvi, 162–66 ("[Constant] . . . prized negative liberty beyond any modern writer.").

4. Constant, "De la liberté."

5. "Commerce makes arbitrary authority easier to evade, because it changes the nature of property, which becomes by that change almost unreachable." Constant, *De l'esprit de conquête et de l'usurpation: dans leurs rapports avec la civilisation européenne* (1814). My parents repeated to me a Central European saying, "Geld allein macht nicht glücklich—man musst es in der Schweiz haben" (Money alone does not make for happiness. You have to have it in Switzerland). "In Constant's view what characterizes our modern world are commerce and the production of goods, activities which need peace among nations and the maximum personal liberty to be carried out successfully. The rights of individuals to self-expression, to property and to privacy have therefore become essential in modern societies." Wood, *Benjamin Constant*, pp. 205–6.

6. He approached John Adams, the then United States ambassador to the Court of St. James's, to explore this possibility.

7. See Ludwig von Mises, *Human Action* (New Haven: Yale University Press, 1949) p. 143: "Society is nothing but the combination of individuals for cooperative effort. It exists nowhere else than in the actions of individual men."

8. See Immanuel Kant, *Groundwork of the Metaphysics of Morals*, H. J. Paton, ed. and trans., 3d ed. (New York: Harper Torchbooks, 1956), p. 116, declaring that "to every rational being possessed of a will we must also lend the Idea of freedom as the only one under which he can act."

9. See Thomas Nagel, *The Possibility of Altruism* (Oxford: Clarendon, 1970); John Rawls, *Political Liberalism*, 2d ed. (New York: Columbia University Press, 2005), p. 51: "Every interest is an interest of a self (agent), but not every interest is in benefits to the self that has it."

10. For one exploration of the sufficient and necessary conditions for coercion, see Robert Nozick, "Coercion," in *Philosophy, Science, and Method: Essays in Honor of Ernest Nagel*, Sidney Morgenbesser et al., eds. (New York: St. Martin's, 1969), p. 440.

11. According to the charter's preamble, Quebec's National Assembly, "recogniz[ing] that Quebecers wish to see the quality and influence of the French language assured, [resolved] to make of French the language of Government and the Law, as well as the normal and everyday language of work, instruction, communication, commerce and business." Charter of the French Language, Preamble, R.S.Q. C-11 (1977). The charter is also commonly referred to as Bill 101.

12. William Johnson, "Latest Ploy by Quebec Language Police Tries the Patients: Elderly Chinese Must Be Treated by French-Speaking Nurses," *Financial Post*, July 31, 1998, p. 1; Paul Amyn, "Pardon My French: Quebec Man Who Took Immersion Here Can't Send Son to English School," *Winnipeg Free Press*, Mar. 7, 2004, p. A3; Stefanie

Arduini, "Unilingual Doll Can't Be Bought in Quebec," *National Post*, Dec. 11, 2003, p. A2; *Financial Post*, Dec. 24, 1997, p. 1; Mark Bourrie, "Row Escalates with Quebec Language Police: Newspaper Vows to Defy Order to Hand Over Photos," *Toronto Star*, May 25, 1998, p. A7.

13. After more than a year, the Quebec Superior Court held that the Montreal Chinese Hospital could indeed make Chinese-language skills a job requirement for a portion of its nursing staff. See Hôpital Chinois de Montréal c. S.C.F.P., section locale 2948, [2000] R.J.D.T. 64, 1999 CarswellQue 3740 (1999). As the result of a 2005 Supreme Court of Canada ruling in a related case, *Solski (Tutor of) v. Québec*, [2005] 1 S.C.R. 201, the Ukrainian father can now send his son to Quebec public English school.

14. Charles Taylor sees the charter as an issue of survival for the francophone community: "It is not just a matter of having the French language available for those who might choose it. . . . It also involves making sure that there is a community of people here in the future that will want to avail itself of the opportunity to use the French language." Charles Taylor, "The Politics of Recognition," in *Multiculturalism: Examining the Politics of Recognition*, Amy Gutmann, ed. (Princeton, N.J.: Princeton University Press, 1994), pp. 25, 58. See also Charter of the French Language, Preamble.

15. In *Chaoulli v. Quebec (Attorney General)*, 2005 S.C.C. 35, 29272, [2005] S.C.J. No. 33 QUICKLAW (June 9, 2005), the Supreme Court of Canada held that the ban on private health insurance violated Quebec's Charter of Human Rights and Freedoms. Clifford Krauss, "As Canada's Slow-Motion Public Health System Falters, Private Medical Care Is Surging," *New York Times*, Feb. 28, 2006, p. A3.

16. "America's 11 Most Endangered Historic Places 2004," available at www.nationaltrust.org/11Most/2004/vermont.html.

17. Cf. Edward L. Glaeser & Matthew E. Kahn, *Sprawl and Urban Growth*, National Bureau of Economic Research Working Paper No. 9733, 2003, explaining urban "sprawl" as substantially the result of consumer demand for larger housing lots and increased use of automobiles.

18. See generally A. O. Hirschman, *Exit, Voice, and Loyalty: Responses to Decline in Firms, Organizations, and States* (Cambridge, Mass.: Harvard University Press, 1970).

19. Robert Reich, secretary of labor from 1993 to 1997, makes this very point: "The problem is, the choices we make in the market don't fully reflect our values as workers or as citizens. I didn't want our community bookstore in Cambridge, Mass., to close (as it did last fall), yet I still bought lots of books from Amazon.com. In addition, we may not see the larger bargain when our own job or community isn't directly at stake. I don't like what's happening to airline workers, but I still try for the cheapest fare I can get." Robert B. Reich, op-ed, "Don't Blame Wal-Mart," *New York Times*, Feb. 28, 2005, p. 19.

CHAPTER 2.

LIBERTY AND ITS COMPETITORS

Epigraph: John Julius Norwich, *A History of Venice* (New York: Knopf, 1982), pp. 492–93. There is a painting of the entry of Henry and his entourage into the church of S. Nicolo by Vicentino in the Sala delle Quattro Porte in the Doges' Palace.

1. This quote is widely attributed to Proust. See "What People Say About Venice," The Web Site of Venice, www.venetia.it/s_dic_eng.htm.

2. Edward Gibbon, *The Decline and Fall of the Roman Empire,* Hans-Friedrich Mueller, ed. (New York: Random House, 2003), p. 604.

3. Arther Ferrill, "Attilla at Châlons," *Quarterly Journal of Military History* (Summer 1989): 48, 51.

4. Brigid Brophy, *Mozart the Dramatist: A New View of Mozart, His Operas, and His Age* (London: Faber & Faber, 1964), pp. 38, 43: "And it is not difficult to read both the prodigies of muscular exertion [by the athlete] and the prodigies of breath control [by the coloratura diva] as metaphors of virtuoso performance in bed. . . .The auditors, who can perhaps sing but cannot sing like *that* . . . and the performers' virtuosity is of a kind precisely calculated to figure to the unconscious as a metaphor of sexual virtuosity, since the fluctuation of lovers' breathing is the indication of sexual intercourse which children most commonly contrive to eavesdrop."

5. Elaine Scarry, *On Beauty and Being Just* (Princeton, N.J.: Princeton University Press, 1999), p. 105.

6. See Thucydides, *The History of the Peloponnesian War,* Book 3, Charles Forster Smith, trans. (Cambridge, Mass.: Harvard/Loeb, 1953).

7. "She [Cleopatra] would not be stripped of her royalty and conveyed to face a jeering triumph: no humble woman she." Horace, *Odes and Epodes,* I. 37, Niall Rudd, ed. and trans. (Cambridge, Mass.: Harvard/Loeb, 2004), p. 95.

8. See Amartya Sen, *Rationality and Freedom* (Cambridge, Mass.: Harvard University Press, 2002), p. 395, speaking of an understanding of liberty that requires "*not merely* that the individual get what he *would* choose *but also* that he get it *through* choosing it himself."

9. See John Rawls, *A Theory of Justice* (Cambridge, Mass.: Harvard University Press, 1971), pp. 567–77: "We can say first that, in a well-ordered society, being a good person (and in particular having an effective sense of justice) is indeed a good for that person."

10. See Ludwig Wittgenstein, *Philosophical Investigations,* 3d ed., G.E.M. Anscombe, trans. (New York: McMillan, 1958), p. 85e.

11. Isaiah Berlin, "Two Concepts of Liberty," in *The Proper Study of Mankind,* p. 197.

12. Abraham Lincoln, "Fragment on Slavery" (attributed date: July 1, 1854), in The Collected Works of Abraham Lincoln, vol. 2, Roy P. Basler, ed. (New Brunswick, N.J.: Rutgers University Press, 1953), pp. 222–23 (emphases in original). Thanks to William Stuntz for the quote.

13. See *The Works of Jeremy Bentham,* vol. 9, John Bowring, ed. (New York: Russell & Russell, 1962), pp. 5–8; John Stuart Mill, *Utilitarianism, Liberty, and Representative Government* (New York: Dutton, 1951), pp. 51–80.

14. See, e.g., David DeGrazia, "On the Question of Personhood Beyond *Homo sapiens,*" in *In Defense of Animals: The Second Wave,* Peter Singer ed. (Blackwell, 2006), pp. 40, 44–46, arguing that both dolphins and apes "act intentionally" and that dolphins exhibit "a high degree of deliberateness and/or rationality"; Francine Patterson and

Wendy Gordon, "The Case for the Personhood of Gorillas," in *The Great Ape Project,* Paola Cavalieri and Peter Singer, eds. (New York: St. Martin's, 1993), pp. 58–59, describing Koko, a lowland gorilla with a "working vocabulary" of over 500 American Sign Language signs, who achieved scores between 85 and 95 on the Stanford-Binet Intelligence Test.

15. For a discussion of these difficulties, see Martha C. Nussbaum, *Frontiers of Justice: Disability, Nationality, Species Membership* (Cambridge, Mass.: Harvard University Press, 2006).

16. In *Sovereign Virtue: The Theory and Practice of Equality* (Cambridge, Mass.: Harvard University Press, 2000), pp. 120–83, Ronald Dworkin proposes a brilliant and intricate conception of distributional equality, what he calls "equality of resources," according to which, he believes, "liberty becomes an aspect of equality rather than . . . an independent political ideal potentially in conflict with it." What he says elsewhere in the book, however, in his analysis of the conflict in respect to medical care, leads me to doubt whether he has indeed succeeded in satisfactorily squaring this circle. At pp. 172–80, Dworkin proposes to "reconcile liberty and equality in the real world of practical and imperfect politics." He assumes, for instance, that if wealth were properly distributed, no constraints on private medicine would be justified. "But the government may nevertheless abolish private medicine as part of a program in search of equality." And he assures us that "fundamental liberties are not put in jeopardy by my argument here, even in a deeply inegalitarian society." His example of such a fundamental liberty is that of homosexuals to "sexual intimacy." I agree that this is such a fundamental liberty; see Chapter 5.

17. In 2000 the ratio of income between the top and bottom 10 percent of earners in Sweden was 6.2; the ratio between the top and bottom 20 percent was 4.0. In the same year, the equivalent ratios in the United States were 15.9 and 8.4, respectively; in 1999, the United Kingdom had ratios of 13.8 and 7.2, respectively. According to the widely used Gini index, scaled between 0 (perfect equality) and 100 (perfect inequality), Sweden scored 25.0, the United States 40.8, and the United Kingdom 36.0. United Nations, *Human Development Report,* p. 270, table 15, available at hdr.undp.org/reports/global/2005/pdf/hdr05_HDI.pdf.

18. Scarry, *On Beauty,* p 98.

19. See Immanuel Kant, *The Metaphysical Elements of Justice,* John Ladd, trans. (Indianapolis: Bobbs-Merrill, 1965), p. 35: "Every action is just [right] that in itself or in its maxim is such that the freedom of the will of each can coexist together with the freedom of everyone in accordance with a universal law." See also Rawls, *A Theory of Justice,* p. 60: "Each person is to have an equal right to the most extensive basic liberty compatible with a similar liberty for others." The "final" statement of this "first principle" differs slightly: "Each person is to have an equal right to the most extensive total system of equal basic liberties compatible with a similar system of liberty for all" (p. 250). For a later version of this formula, see John Rawls, *Justice as Fairness: A Restatement* (Cambridge, Mass.: Harvard University Press, 2001), pp. 42–50.

20. This saying is widely attributed to Holmes, who in *The Common Law* discusses *Brown v. Kendall,* 60 Mass. 292 (1850). In that case, the Supreme Court of Massachusetts

held the defendant, who had severely injured the plaintiff's eye with a stick while trying to separate the men's fighting dogs, to an "ordinary care" standard, meaning "that
kind and degree of care, which prudent and cautious men would use, such as is
required by the exigency of the case, and such as is necessary to guard against prob-
able danger" (p. 296). The defendant, in other words, was liable to the plaintiff if he
used less than ordinary care. This standard is ubiquitous in the law: we must take others into account.

21. I have asked this question before. See Charles Fried, "Is Liberty Possible," in *The Tan-
ner Lectures on Human Values,* vol. 3 (Cambridge, Eng.: Cambridge University Press,
1982), p. 89.

Chapter 3.
Liberty and Rights

1. I refer to the idea of freedom as capability that is most fully developed by Amartya
Sen and Martha Nussbaum. See Amartya Sen, *Development as Freedom* (New York:
Knopf, 1999). Nussbaum has contributed extensively to the literature on capabilities.
One primary contribution to Sen's approach is her list of ten "central human capabil-
ities," which include life; bodily health; bodily integrity; senses, imagination, and
thought; emotions; practical reason; affiliation; other species (living with and having
concern for animals, plants, and nature); play; and control over one's political and
material environment. See Martha Nussbaum, *Women and Human Development: The
Capabilities Approach* (Cambridge, Eng.: Cambridge University Press, 2000); Martha
C. Nussbaum, "Capabilities as Fundamental Entitlements: Sen and Social Justice,"
Feminist Economics (July-Nov. 2003): 33, 41–42.

2. See O. W. Holmes, Jr., *The Common Law* (London: Macmillan, 1887), p. 3.

3. I have written a book about this: Charles Fried, *Contract as Promise* (Cambridge,
Mass.: Harvard University Press, 1981).

4. See, e.g., Jean Piaget, *The Moral Judgment of the Child* (New York: Free Press 1965);
Janet W. Astington, "Children's Understanding of the Speech Act of Promising," *Journal of Child Language* 157 (1988): 15, tracking children's understanding of the concept of "promise" between ages five and thirteen, in particular finding that younger
children equate "promise" with "telling the truth," while by age nine most children
can distinguish between promise and prediction.

5. See Barbara H. Fried, *The Progressive Assault on Laissez Faire: Robert Hale and the First
Law and Economics Movement* (Cambridge, Mass.: Harvard University Press, 1998);
Cass R. Sunstein, *Free Markets and Social Justice* (New York: Oxford University Press,
1997).

6. See Lon L. Fuller, *The Morality of Law* (New Haven, Conn.: Yale University Press,
1969), pp. 124–25.

7. See F. A. Hayek, *Law, Legislation, and Liberty: A New Statement of the Liberal Principles of Justice and Political Economy* (Chicago: University of Chicago Press, 1979),
and Friedrich A. Hayek, *The Constitution of Liberty* (Chicago: University of Chicago
Press, 1960).

8. See Chapter 1, note 14.
9. Richard M. Titmuss, *The Gift Relationship: From Human Blood to Social Policy* (London: London School of Economics, 1997).
10. John Locke, *Two Treatises of Government,* Thomas Hollis, ed. (London: A. Millar et al., 1764), bk. 2, ch. V, section 27. To the same effect, see Immanuel Kant, *The Metaphysical Elements of Justice,* John Ladd, trans. (Indianapolis: Bobbs-Merrill, 1965), pp. 51–72; and Immanuel Kant, *The Science of Right* (1790), sections 15, 17.
11. This argument has been taken up by other philosophers and given a less austere, more affirmative force. See, e.g., Kant, *Science of Right*, sections 18–21. Hegel presents a more romantic view, described as the "theory that individuals have a right to possess some minimal amount of property in order to express their freedom by embodying their will in external objects. It is a more positive conception of the right to property than Locke's theory, which is mainly negative because it depends on freedom from interference in the acquisition and use of property." Liam Murphy and Thomas Nagel, *The Myth of Ownership* (New York: Oxford University Press, 2002), p. 45 (citing G.W.F. Hegel, *Philosophy of Right*, sections 41–53). Obviously, I have borrowed the title of this section from Murphy and Nagel.
12. Jeremy Waldron, "Homelessness and the Issue of Freedom," *UCLA Law Review* 295 (1991): 39, 296–300.
13. He may be able to pay very little because of the relative urgency of my need—but if I can unionize with all others in my situation, we may be able to make his need as urgent as ours.
14. G. A. Cohen has developed the critique of Lockean rights in *Self-Ownership, Freedom, and Equality* (Cambridge, Eng.: Cambridge University Press, 1995) and "Freedom and Money: An Essay in Grateful Memory of Isaiah Berlin," www.utdt.edu/departamentos/derecho/publicaciones/rtj1/pdf/finalfreedom.pdf.
15. Robert Nozick, *Anarchy, State, and Utopia* (New York: Basic, 1974), pp. 174–78.
16. Herman Melville, *Moby-Dick; or, the Whale* (Berkeley: University of California Press, 1979), p. 406.
17. Murphy and Nagel, *Myth,* p. 63, n. 3.
18. Ibid., pp. 63–66.
19. Ibid., pp. 66, 75.
20. Ibid., pp. 65, 64. For a more general version of Murphy and Nagel's thesis, see Stephen Holmes and Cass R. Sunstein, *The Cost of Rights: Why Liberty Depends on Taxes* (New York: Norton, 1999), arguing that all rights are political because they depend on government action—e.g., police protection—for their effective realization.
21. Plutarch, *The Lives of the Noble Grecians and Romans*, vol. 2, Arthur Hugh Clough, trans. (New York: Modern Library, 1992), p. 148.
22. This is a reappearance of the Hobbesian argument that a sovereign, no matter how dreadful, is preferable to the "war of all against all" that would exist without it. This particular way of passing from whatever is to what has a moral claim on us has been refuted too often to require attention here. Briefly: It is far from obvious that some, at least, would not prefer to take their chances in that war, at least to some regimes. And then it is a fair question why we should accept as a baseline the existence of any

regime at all. Is it because no argument is available to insist on the moral preferabil-
ity of any one regime over another? And so it is any regime against none at all. This
last contention assumes the answer to the question of whether argument might not
provide some criteria for choosing among, or at least eliminating some, alternative
regimes or systems of law.

23. Though not secure against disease, natural disaster, or bad luck, which takes us back
to the discussion in Chapter 2.

CHAPTER 4.
LIBERTY OF THE MIND

1. 44 *Liquormart, Inc. v. Rhode Island*, 517 U.S. 484 (1996).
2. Ludwig Wittenstein, *Tractatus Logico-Philosophicus* (London: Routledge, 2000), section 7.
3. May you then write your private diary, your unpublished novel, your correspondence
to friends abroad in English? Under the Quebec language law, you may do that and a
good deal more. But I would say that is only because the Quebec regime is after all a
decent and liberal one, unwilling to follow the implications of its strictures. The hope
of the law is that if not everyone, if not you, then your children or some increasing
number of those around you will eventually think in French. Otherwise what would
be the point?
4. In the hilarious episode known as the Sokal hoax, Professor Alan Sokal, a theoretical
physicist, submitted a paper entitled "Transgressing the Boundaries: Toward a Trans-
formative Hermeneutics of Quantum Gravity" to *Social Text*, a leading scholarly
journal in cultural studies, the academic field consecrated to the social-construction-
of-everything thesis. Sokal deliberately made his arguments from science drastically,
catastrophically wrong, when they were not simply incoherent. The learned editors of
Social Text accepted his submission for publication in a special double edition devoted
to defending cultural studies against the charge that their treatment of science was
ignorant and incompetent. Sokal thus convicted the editors—leaders in their field—
not just of stupidity and ignorance but, as the philosopher Paul Boghossian has pointed
out, of being politicians "prepared to let agreement with [their] ideological orientation
trump every other criterion for publication, including something as basic as sheer intel-
ligibility." Paul A. Boghossian, "What the Sokal Hoax Ought to Teach Us," *Times Lit-
erary Supplement*, Dec. 13, 1996, pp. 14–15. For a serious discussion of this position,
see Thomas Nagel, *The Last Word* (New York: Oxford University Press, 1997).
5. Nagel has addressed the social construction view head on: "The objection that has to
be answered, here as elsewhere, is that . . . unconditioned, nonrelative judgment is
an illusion—that we cannot, merely by stepping back and taking ourselves as objects
of contemplation, find a secure platform from which such judgment is possible. On
this view whatever we do . . . will still inevitably be a manifestation of our individual
or social nature, not the deliverance of impersonal reason—for there is no such thing.
But I do not believe that such a conclusion can be established. . . . The subjectivist
would have to show that all purportedly rational judgments about what people have

reason to do are really expressions of rationally unmotivated desires or dispositions of the person making the judgment—desires or dispositions to which normative assessment has no application." Nagel, *Last Word*, pp. 110–11. See also Immanuel Kant, *Critique of Practical Reason*, Lewis White Beck, trans. (New York: Mcmillan, 1985), pp. 92–110; Immanuel Kant, *Groundwork for the Metaphysics of Morals*, Allen W. Wood, ed. and trans. (New Haven: Yale University Press, 2002), p. 69: "With the idea of freedom the concept of *autonomy* is inseparably bound up, but with the latter the universal principle of morality, which in the idea grounds all actions of *rational* beings just as the natural law grounds all appearances."

6. See Nagel, *Last Word*, pp. 55–76 ("Logic").

7. Ivan Illich, "Vernacular Values," in *Shadow Work* (1981), pp. 27, 41: "Silent reading is a recent invention." My five-year-old grandson found it quite hard to understand that I was reading to myself without even moving my lips.

8. What is perhaps our most fervent communication, however, remains largely silent: prayer. Often communicating our most honest and intimate thought, it is expression rarely revealed.

9. *West Virginia State Bd. of Educ. v. Barnette*, 319 U.S. 624, 642 (1943).

10. Liam Murphy and Thomas Nagel, *The Myth of Ownership* (New York: Oxford University Press, 2002), p. 64.

11. *Hague v. Comm. for Indus. Org.*, 307 U.S. 496, 515 (1939).

12. The phrase "a New Deal for speech" is Cass Sunstein's. He urges doing the same thing for free speech theory that Roosevelt's New Deal did for property rights and freedom of contracts. Cass R. Sunstein, *Democracy and the Problem of Free Speech* (New York: Free Press, 1993), pp. 17–52; Cass R. Sunstein, *The Partial Constitution* (Cambridge, Mass.: Harvard University Press, 1993), pp. 197–231; Cass Sunstein, *Republic.com* (Princeton, N.J.: Princeton University Press, 2001), pp. 125–66.

13. See *Pruneyard Shopping Ctr. v. Robins*, 447 U.S. 74, 83 (1980), finding that a private shopping mall that "covers several city blocks, contains numerous separate business establishments, and is open to the public at large" had no federal constitutional right to deny access to the public for purposes of "free expression and petition[ing]"; *Int'l Soc'y for Krishna Consciousness, Inc. v. Lee*, 505 U.S. 672 (1992), finding that airport terminals are not public forums; *Benefit v. City of Cambridge*, 424 Mass. 918, 919 (1997), holding that a city ordinance banning panhandling in "areas to which the general public is invited" is unconstitutional; Yochai Benkler and Lawrence Lessig, "Net Gains," *New Republic*, Dec. 14, 1998, p. 15, arguing that technology may soon render FCC control of the airwaves—a "monopol[y] over valuable speech resources"— unconstitutional.

14. For an account of the principles of American free speech constitutional doctrine, see Charles Fried, *Saying What the Law Is: The Constitution in the Supreme Court* (Cambridge, Mass.: Harvard University Press, 2004), ch. 4.

15. Compare *Ward v. Rock Against Racism*, 491 U.S. 781 (1989), upholding a city regulation requiring performers in a city park bandshell to use a city-provided sound system and noting that "even in a public forum the government may impose reasonable restrictions on the time, place, or manner of protected speech," with *Collin v. Smith*,

578 F.2d 1197, 1207 (7th Cir. 1978), invalidating three village ordinances targeted at preventing a Nazi party contingent from marching in front of the village hall, finding that "no justifiable substantial privacy interest [allows the village to declare itself] a privacy zone that may be sanitized from the offensiveness of Nazi ideology and symbols."

16. Cf. *Meyer v. Nebraska*, 262 U.S. 390 (1923), declaring unconstitutional a Nebraska statute requiring English-only education in all schools—public, private, or parochial—in the state; *Bartels v. Iowa*, 262 U.S. 404 (1923), similarly invalidating an Iowa statute prohibiting foreign-language education below the eighth grade.

17. See Sunstein, *Democracy and Free Speech*, p. 36: "Governmental rules lie behind and create rights of property, contract, and tort"; Sunstein, *Republic.com*, pp. 128–31: "This gift [the government's decision to give existing broadcast owners a right to produce digital television for "free"] from the public . . . is simply the most recent . . . way in which government, and law, are responsible for the rights of those who own and operate radio and television stations." See also Owen M. Fiss, *The Irony of Free Speech* (Cambridge, Mass.: Harvard University Press, 1996); Morton J. Horwitz, "Foreword: The Constitution of Change: Legal Fundamentality Without Fundamentalism," *Harvard Law Review* 30, 109 (1993): 107, lamenting the "Lochnerization of the First Amendment."

18. See Cass Sunstein, "The Future of Free Speech," *Little Magazine*, Mar.-Apr. 2001, www.littlemag.com/mar-apr01/cass.html, p. 10: "If we believed that the Constitution gives all owners of speech outlets an unabridgeable right to decide what appears on 'their' outlets, the . . . government could [not regulate their output]. But why should we believe that? Broadcasters owe their licenses to a government grant, and owners of Websites enjoy their rights of ownership largely because of the law, which creates and enforces property rights"; Owen Fiss, "The Censorship of Television," *Northwestern University Law Review* 1215, 1223 (1999): 93: "Every media organization receives significant benefits from the state. Some such benefits can be found in the laws of contract, property, and corporations, and in the provision of services such as police and fire protection that are generally available to all citizens."

19. *Voting with Dollars: A New Paradigm for Campaign Finance* (New Haven: Yale University Press, 2002), pp. 12–24.

20. Murphy and Nagel, *Myth of Ownership*, pp. 63, 64.

21. See Robert C. Post, "Community and the First Amendment," *Arizona State Law Journal* 473 (1997): 29: "The claim of autonomy, although it is dressed in the language of speech, is ultimately merely a variant of the generic claim to human freedom. Precisely because such a claim can be invoked always and everywhere, it is very dilute. It is outweighed every time the state must regulate behavior. For this reason autonomy interests in speech are easily overridden by competing interests."

22. *Wisconsin v. Yoder*, 406 U.S. 205, 211-12 (1972).

23. Ibid., p. 245 (Douglas, J., dissenting in part): "It is the future of the student, not the future of the parents, that is imperiled by today's decision."

24. *W. Va. State Bd. of Educ. v. Barnette*, 319 U.S. 624 (1943); *Pierce v. Soc'y of Sisters*, 268 U.S. 510 (1925); *Meyer v. Nebraska*, 262 U.S. 390 (1923).

25. Edmund Gosse, *Father and Son: A Study of Two Temperaments* (London: Oxford University Press, 1974).

CHAPTER 5.
SEX

Epigraph: Nicolas de Chamfort, *Maximes et Pensées: Caractères et Anecdotes* (Paris: Gallimard, 1970), section 359, p. 110. It sounds better in French, especially when spoken by a beautiful woman of the world in Jean Renoir's *La Règle du Jeu*.

1. Liam Murphy and Thomas Nagel, *The Myth of Ownership* (New York: Oxford University Press, 2002), p. 65.

2. Such a tendency has been ascribed to Rawls's famous original position behind the veil of ignorance, where we choose our principles without knowing our physical circumstances, our contingent ties, our talents, tastes, and character. John Rawls, *A Theory of Justice* (Cambridge, Mass.: Harvard/Belknap, 1971), pp. 17–22.

3. See Pope Benedict XVI's first encyclical, *Deus Caritas Est* (January 25, 2006).

4. Catharine A. MacKinnon, *Toward a Feminist Theory of the State* (Cambridge, Mass.: Harvard University Press, 1989), p. 195.

5. See Andrea Dworkin, *Intercourse* (London: Secker & Warburg, 1987), p. 122: "A human being has a body that is inviolate; and when it is violated, it is abused. A woman has a body that is penetrated in intercourse: permeable, its corporeal solidness a lie. The discourse of male truth . . . calls that penetration *violation*. . . . *Violation* is a synonym for intercourse. At the same time, the penetration is taken to be a use, not an abuse; a normal use; it is appropriate to enter her, to push into ("violate") the boundaries of her body. She is human, of course, but by a standard that does not include physical privacy. . . . To keep a man out altogether and for a lifetime is deviant in the extreme, a psychopathology, a repudiation of the way in which she is expected to manifest her humanity."

6. See Karl Marx and Frederick Engels, *Communist Manifesto*, in *Collected Works*, vol. 6 (New York: International, 1976), pp. 476–519.

7. Richard M. Titmuss, *The Gift Relationship* (London: London School of Economics, 1997), p. 314: "The commercialisation of blood and donor relationships represses the expression of altruism, erodes the sense of community, . . . and results in situations in which proportionately more and more blood is supplied by the poor, the unskilled, the unemployed, Negroes and other low income groups. . . . Commercial markets are much more likely to distribute contaminated blood." See also Margaret Jane Radin, *Contested Commodities* (Cambridge, Mass.: Harvard University Press, 1996), pp. 95–114, responding to Titmuss by advancing and exploring the idea of "incomplete commodification."

8. Titmuss, *Gift Relationship*, pp. 307–8.

9. Frederick Schauer, "Speech and 'Speech'—Obscenity and 'Obscenity': An Exercise in the Interpretation of Constitutional Language," *Georgia Law Journal* 899, 922–26 (1979): 67. See Eric A. Posner, "Law and the Emotions," *Georgia Law Journal* 1977, 2012 (2001): 89: "Suppose [a person] feels disgusted whenever he sees adults of the

same sex holding hands. This person might be willing to pay for laws that discourage such behavior because he wishes to avoid the sensation of disgust. The question is whether this person's preference should count, just as it would surely count if he were objecting to a noxious odor caused by pollution."

10. Kwame Anthony Appiah, *Cosmopolitanism: Ethics in a World of Strangers* (New York: Norton, 2006), p. 77.

11. See Immanuel Kant, *The Metaphysics of Morals*, Mary Gregor, trans. (Cambridge, Eng.: Cambridge University Press, 1991), section 25, p. 96.

12. Ibid., sections 24–26, pp. 96–98, equating "natural" sex with that "by which procreation of a being of the same kind is possible"; Immanuel Kant, *Lectures on Ethics,* Peter Heath, trans. (Cambridge, Eng.: Cambridge University Press, 2001), pp. 160–61.

13. Sociobiologists see in all this a device that has recruited our instincts into the Darwinian project of producing and caring for future generations. See, e.g., Edward O. Wilson, *Sociobiology: The New Synthesis* (Cambridge, Mass.: Harvard/Belknap, 2000), pp. 547–48, detailing several traits of human sexuality that "cement the close marriage bonds that are basic to human social life." So be it. The two explanations are not incompatible.

14. See Martha C. Nussbaum, *Hiding from Humanity: Disgust, Shame, and the Law* (Princeton, N.J.: Princeton University Press, 2004), pp. 71–123; William Ian Miller, *The Anatomy of Disgust* (Cambridge, Mass.: Harvard University Press, 1997); William N. Eskridge, Jr., "Body Politics: *Lawrence v. Texas* and the Constitution of Disgust and Contagion," *Florida Law Review* 1011, 1023 (2005): 57; Richard A. Posner, *Sex and Reason* (Cambridge, Mass.: Harvard University Press, 1992), p. 98, listing as "deviant" sex "masturbation, homosexuality, voyeurism, exhibitionism, seduction of young children, and fetishism."

15. Here I paraphrase Justice Jackson in *Youngstown Sheet & Tube Co. v. Sawyer*, 343 U.S. 579, 634 (1952) (Jackson, J., concurring in the judgment).

16. This is a version of Hegel's famous dialectic of the master and slave, in which Hegel shows that the master demeans his own humanity by holding another in slavery. See G.W.F. Hegel, *Phenomenology of Spirit*, A. V. Miller, trans. (Oxford: Oxford University Press, 1977), pp. 110–18.

17. Nozick explains the difference between coercive threats and noncoercive offers as the former, if carried out, resulting in worsening of the "normal and expected course of events," and the latter resulting in an improvement over the normally expected outcome. Or, more succinctly, an offer improves a person's set of options, a threat limits it. See Robert Nozick, "Coercion," in *Philosophy, Science, and Method*, Morgenbesser et al., eds. (New York: St. Martin's, 1969), pp. 440, 447–53.

18. Michael J. Sandel, "Markets, Morals, and Civic Life," *Bulletin of the American Academy of Arts & Sciences* 58 (Summer 2005): 6.

19. I put to one side the cases in which someone bribes the judges or others who are put in that position in order to render a judgment on the merits. They are like the corrupt policeman.

20. Appiah, *Cosmopolitanism*, p. 111.

21. *Lawrence v. Texas*, 539 U.S. 558 (2003), overruling *Bowers v. Hardwick*, 478 U.S. 186 (1986).

22. See Leon R. Kass, *Life, Liberty and the Defense of Dignity: The Challenge for Bioethics* (San Francisco: Encounter, 2002), ch. 5, pp. 177–219.

23. Galway Kinnell, "After Making Love We Hear Footsteps," in *Mortal Acts, Mortal Wounds* (Boston: Houghton Mifflin, 1980). Kass's council includes this poem—with introductory commentary posing questions such as "What enables the parents to see [the child] as a blessing, as 'this blessing,' and as a 'gift of love'—and do they see rightly?"—as part of its "bookshelf" collection, *Being Human: Readings from the President's Council on Bioethics,* available at www.bioethics.gov/bookshelf/reader/chapter6 .html.

CHAPTER 6.

BACK TO WORK

1. Liam Murphy and Thomas Nagel, *The Myth of Ownership* (New York: Oxford University Press, 2002), pp. 64, 65.

2. See Robert Nozick, *Anarchy, State, and Utopia* (New York: Basic, 1974), pp. 160–64.

3. Ibid., p. 169: "Taxation of earnings from labor is on a par with forced labor."

4. Compare Hegel's dialectic of the master and slave, Chapter 6.

5. This is an argument that Kant makes in the *Groundwork* and is related to Rawls's veil-of-ignorance argument.

6. I borrow from my essay "Markets, Law, and Democracy," *Journal of Democracy* 11 (July 2000): 5, 7.

7. The Libertarian Nation Foundation makes such a claim, working toward "the day when coercive institutions of government can be replaced by voluntary institutions of civil mutual consent, by developing clear and believable descriptions of those voluntary institutions, and by building a community of people who share confidence in these descriptions." See libertariannation.org/index.php.

8. Martin Feldstein, *Income Inequality, and Poverty*, National Bureau of Economic Research Working Paper 6770, Oct. 1998.

9. Legislative Council Secretariat, *Fact Sheet*, www.legco.gov.hk/yr04-05/english/ sec/library/0405fs07e.pdf. These figures are only approximately comparable, as each country may use different methods of collecting the underlying data.

10. The property owner owns land either to the low-water mark or to 100 rods (1,650 feet) seaward of the high-water mark, whichever is less. Further, the public enjoys easements for the purposes of "fishing, fowling, and navigation." See *Opinion of the Justices to the House of Representatives*, 365 Mass. 681 (1974). For a history of tideland rights in Massachusetts, see *Trio Algarvio, Inc. v. Comm'r of the Dep't of Envtl. Prot.*, 440 Mass. 94, 97–101 (2003).

11. See, e.g., *Idaho v. Coeur D'Alene Tribe*, 521 U.S. 261, 284 (1997): "'In England . . . it has been treated as settled that the title in the soil of the sea, or of arms of the sea, below ordinary high water mark, is in the King . . . and that this title, *jus privatum*, whether in the King or in a subject, is held subject to the public right, *jus publicum*, of navigation and fishing.' Not surprisingly, American law adopted as its own much of the English law respecting navigable waters, including the principle that submerged

lands are held for a public purpose." For an overview of the property rights in the original colonies, see *Shively v. Bowlby*, 152 U.S. 1, 18–26 (1894).

12. In 1974 the Massachusetts legislature considered allowing for a "public on-foot free
    right-of-passage" between the mean high-water line and extreme low-water line—
    essentially, anyone could walk on any beach. Massachusetts's highest court advised
    the legislature that this would amount to taking private property, since upland
    landowners would be divested of a right to prevent physical invasion of their property,
    a right currently tempered only by allowances for "fishing, fowling, and navigation."
    Hence, the statute would be unconstitutional unless it provided for adequate com-
    pensation to the landowners. See *Opinion of Justices*, 365 Mass. 681 (1974).

13. Cf. Randy E. Barnett, *Restoring the Lost Constitution: The Presumption of Liberty*
    (Princeton, N.J.: Princeton University Press, 2004).

14. Bracton, *Bracton on the Laws and Customs of England*, vol. 2, attributed to Henry of
    Bratton, c. 1210–1268, p. 58, available at 140.247.226.46/bracton//index.htm.

15. See *Rancho Viejo, LLC v. Norton*, 323 F.3d 1062 (D.C. Cir. 2003).

16. See Genesis 1:26.

17. Even a very conservative judge writing at a very conservative time understood this: "A
    person has no property, no vested interest, in any rule of the common law. That is only
    one of the forms of municipal law, and is no more sacred than any other. Rights of
    property which have been created by the common law cannot be taken away without
    due process; but the law itself, as a rule of conduct, may be changed at the will . . .
    of the legislature, unless prevented by constitutional limitations." Second Employee
    Liability Cases, 223 U.S. 1 50 (1917), quoting *Munn v. Illinois*, 84 U.S. 113, 134
    (1876) (Van Devanter, J.).

18. There are lively debates and immense literature about the application of the norms
    of intellectual property in cyberspace. See, e.g., Lawrence Lessig, "Innovating Copy-
    right," *Cardozo Arts and Entertainment Law Journal* 611, 623 (2002): 20: "We have to
    free ourselves from the idea that our culture is the property of others. We as creators,
    as people empowered by digital technologies in ways no one ever imagined before,
    should have the right to build, to add, to rip, mix and burn this culture in ways that
    our framers would have found fantastic"; Jonathan Zittrain, "The Copyright Cage,"
    Legal Affairs, July/Aug. 2003, www.legalaffairs.org/issues/July-August-2003/feature_
    zittrain_julaug03.msp: "I hate the effects of copyright on a digital revolution that her-
    alds so much more than the banal ripping off of CD tracks. I hate that creativity is
    metered and parceled to its last ounce of profit. I hate that our technology is hobbled
    beyond its paper and other analog counterparts so that it permits us to view but not
    print, listen but not share, read once but not lend, consume but not create. But I can
    hate this situation without believing that the idea of copyright is fundamentally
    flawed" (emphasis omitted); William W. Fisher III, *Promises to Keep: Technology, Law,
    and the Future of Entertainment* (Stanford, Calif.: Stanford University Press, 2004),
    p. 7: "As Jamie Boyle asks, are kindergarten teachers really supposed to instruct their
    charges that, while 'sharing' toys is commendable, 'sharing' music and movies is
    immoral?"; Recording Industry Association of America, *Music and the Internet*,
    www.riaa.com/issues/music/default.asp: "The possibilities are great for the music

industry: fans, artists, and record companies alike. The opportunities offered by the new technologies seem limitless. At the same time, in taking advantage of those opportunities, it is crucial that the artists who produce the music are not taken advantage of. That's not fair and it will hurt our creative future"; see also Cass Sunstein, *Republic.com* (Princeton, N.J.: Princeton University Press, 2001).

19. See *United States v. Causby*, 328 U.S. 256 (1946), holding, in a claim brought by owners of land lying directly under the flight path of planes using an adjacent military airport, that low-level flights could constitute a taking under the Fifth Amendment.

20. See Murphy and Nagel, *Myth of Ownership*, pp. 130–41; Walter J. Blum and Harry Kalven, Jr., "The Uneasy Case for Progressive Taxation," *University of Chicago Law Review* 417 (1952): 19.

21. Louis Kaplow and Steven Shavell, *Fairness versus Welfare* (Cambridge, Mass.: Harvard University Press, 2002), pp. 31–35.

22. See Randy E. Barnett, *Restoring the Lost Constitution*; F. A. Hayek, *The Road to Serfdom* (London: Routledge, 2001), pp. 75–90.

CHAPTER 7.
THE SPIRIT OF LIBERTY

1. B. Netanyahu, *The Origins of the Inquisition in Fifteenth-Century Spain* (New York: Random House, 1995), pp. 975–80.

2. There is the story about the nun who, asked why she took her bath fully clothed when no one could see her behind a locked door, replied that God could see her. Bertrand Russell, *Unpopular Essays* (London : Routledge, 1995), pp. 86–87. One suspects the real answer is that she could see herself.

3. Stephen Breyer, *Active Liberty: Interpreting Our Democratic Constitution* (New York: Knopf, 2005), p. 55.

4. See Frederick F. Schauer, "Reflections on 'Contemporary Community Standards': The Perpetuation of an Irrelevant Concept in the Law of Obscenity," *North Carolina Law Review* 1, 14–17 (1978): 56; Cass R. Sunstein, "Pornography and the First Amendment," *Duke Law Journal* 589 (1986): 616–17: "The 'message' of pornography is communicated indirectly and not through rational persuasion. The harm it produces cannot easily be countered by more speech because it bypasses the process of public consideration and debate that underlies the concept of the marketplace of ideas." Schauer's view of pornography may be right, but only so far as this justifies regulating public displays. Its private consumption is at least as privileged by liberty as the conduct it depicts. This is not the only front on which these battles are being fought. See my *Saying What the Law Is: The Constitution in the Supreme Court* (Cambridge, Mass.; Harvard University Press, 2004), pp. 102–6.

5. Thomas Nagel, *The Last Word* (New York: Oxford University Press, 1997), pp. 55–76.

6. John Stuart Mill, *On Liberty*, ch. 5: "If the government would make up its mind to require for every child a good education, it might save itself the trouble of providing one. It might leave to parents to obtain the education where and how they pleased."

7. Cf. Edward L. Glaeser and Matthew E. Kahn, *Sprawl and Urban Growth*; Edward L.

Glaeser and Jesse Shapiro, *Is There a New Urbanism?: The Growth of U.S. Cities in the 1990s*, National Bureau of Economic Research Working Paper Series No. 8357 (2001), finding correlations between urban growth and "strong human capital bases," preference for warmer and drier climates, and use of automobiles rather than public transportation.

8. 44 *Liquormart, Inc. v. Rhode Island*, 517 U.S. 484, 516 (1996); *Va. State Bd. of Pharmacy v. Va. Citizens Consumer Council*, 425 U.S. 748 (1976).

9. The Oklahoma scheme was upheld by the Tenth Circuit; *Powers v. Harris,* 379 F.3d 1208 (10th Cir. 2004), *cert. denied*, 125 S. Ct. 1638 (2005). The Sixth Circuit struck down the Tennessee scheme under the Fourteenth Amendment; *Craigmiles v. Giles,* 312 F.3d 220 (6th Cir. 2002).

10. *McCray v. United States,* 195 U.S. 27 (1904).

11. Enrollment in the German social insurance program is mandatory for those with incomes below a certain threshold 45,900 in 2005); those with higher incomes may choose between the public and private plans. British citizens, though required to enroll in the public health program, may purchase supplemental insurance, which allows queue-jumping and citizen choice of physician and hospital. Finally, around 85 percent of French citizens maintain private supplemental insurance. Expenditures on private plans make up about 12 percent of the country's health costs. See Timothy Stoltzfus Jost, "Private or Public Approaches to Insuring the Uninsured: Lessons from International Experience with Private Insurance," *New York University Law Review* 76 (2001): 419, 439, 468–71.

12. Richard H. Thaler and Cass R. Sunstein, "Libertarian Paternalism," *American Economic Review* 93 (2003): 175.

13. *Pierce v. Soc'y of Sisters,* 268 U.S. 510 (1925).

14. The phrase is Joshua Cohen's, paraphrasing Habermas. Referring to the earliest generation of art critics, Habermas says: "They knew of no authority beside that of the better argument"; Jürgen Habermas, *The Structural Transformation of the Public Sphere*, Thomas Burger, trans. (Cambridge, Mass.: MIT Press, 1998), p. 41. Referring to the idea of discourse, Habermas says that "no force except that of the better argument is exercised"; *Legitimation Crisis*, Thomas McCarthy, trans. (Cambridge, Eng.: Polity Press, 1988), p. 108.

15. Robert Nozick, *Philosophical Explanations* (Cambridge, Mass.: Harvard/Belknap, 1981), p. 7.

16. See my *Saying What the Law Is*, pp. 78–142.

17. See Colin Lucas, "Nobles, Bourgeois, and the Origins of the French Revolution," *Past and Present*, Aug. 1973, pp. 84, 118. The principle sounds even earlier: "Yet while as regards the law all men are on an equality for the settlement of their private disputes, as regards the value set on them it is as each man is in any way distinguished that he is preferred to public honours, not because he belongs to a particular class, but because of personal merits; nor, again, on the ground of poverty is a man barred from a public career by obscurity of rank if he but has it in him to do the state a service"; Pericles' Funeral Oration, in Thucydides, *History of the Peloponnesian War*, vol. 2, Charles Forster Smith, trans. (Cambridge, Mass.: Harvard/Loeb, 1969), p. 323.

18. "Nor shall private property be taken for public use, without just compensation"; U.S. Constitution, Amendment V. Under NAFTA, no country may nationalize or expropriate an investment by another country's investor unless doing so (1) for a public purpose; (2) on a nondiscriminatory basis; (3) with due process of law; and (4) upon payment of appropriate compensation; see North American Free Trade Agreement, Dec. 8–17, 1992, U.S.- Can.-Mex., ch. 11, section B, 32 I.L.M. 605, 642–47.

19. UNESCO attempted in the early 1980s to implement the "New World Information Order," purportedly to prevent the spread of misinformation about developing nations. The United States and the UK both withdrew from the organization in protest. Zimbabwe is notorious for its emasculation of the press; see, e.g., Michael Wines, "3 Journalists Flee Zimbabwe, Fearing Arrest After Threats," *New York Times*, Feb. 22, 2005, p. A3.

20. See Richard A. Epstein, *Takings: Private Property and the Power of Eminent Domain* (Cambridge, Mass.: Harvard University Press, 1985); Bruce A. Ackerman, *Private Property and the Constitution* (New Haven, Conn.: Yale University Press, 1977); William A. Fischel, *Regulatory Takings: Law, Economics, and Politics* (Cambridge, Mass.: Harvard University Press, 1998).

21. I develop this metaphor in "The Artificial Reason of the Law or: What Lawyers Know," *Texas Law Review* 60 (1981): 35, 57.

INDEX

natural liberty, 91
natural rights, 80, 85, 91, 92
    liberty of mind as, 94, 152–53
    sex as, 153
Nazis, 104–5, 110
negative externalities, 34, 38
negative taxes, 87
New Deal, 112
New Hampshire, 165
newspapers, 109
New York, N.Y., 26
Nicaragua, 163
Nineteen Eighty-Four (Orwell),
    97
Norwich, John Julius, 41, 42
Nozick, Robert, 82, 86, 146, 147,
    181, 186, 197
Nuremberg Rally, 45
Nussbaum, Martha C., 189, 190,
    196

Office of the French Language,
    167
Oklahoma, 174–75
Old Order Amish, 120, 121
On Beauty and Being Just (Scarry),
    44
On Liberty (Mill), 101, 118
operas, opera companies, 117,
    173–74
opportunity, equality of, 89
Ortega, Daniel, 163
Orwell, George, 97
Othello, 51
Ottoman Empire, 48
ownership:
    "myth of," 85–90, 112, 114,
        152
    pretax, 86
    see also property

pain, property and, 148
Pangloss, 91
Paraguay, inequality in, 151

parents:
    biological, 138–39
    children loved by, 133–34, 139
parks, free speech in, 105, 107
Parliament, British, 104
patrons, patronage, 73
    poverty and, 90
Pericles, 44–45
personal enlistment, 32
philosophers, 65
    of freedom, 132–33
    see also specific philosophers
physics, 100
plays, 114
Pledge of Allegiance, 103, 120
Plymouth Brethren, 121
politics, 114
    orthodoxy in, 103
Pol Pot, 18, 19, 24, 58, 59, 60, 61,
        126, 163, 165
pornography, 110, 114, 129–30
positive externalities, 38
poverty, 90, 115–16
    equality and, 150
power, 17, 94, 99
Prague, 17
pre-law notion, 72
prepolitical rights, 144–45
press, free, 107, 109
    in Quebec, 167
pretax ownership, 86
pretax wealth, 111
price controls, 95–96
principle of liberty, 63–64
privacy:
    liberty and, 103, 113
    sex and, 135–36
Prohibition, 160
property, 64, 69–71, 152–60, 181,
        182
    beachfront, 153–55
    boundary problem and, 82–83,
        135
    as derivative, 88

About the Author

Charles Fried is the Beneficial Professor of Law at Harvard Law School. Born in Prague in 1935, he fled with his family in 1939, first to England and then to the United States. Educated in public and private schools, he received his bachelor's degree from Princeton and law degrees from Oxford and Columbia Universities. After a clerkship on the Supreme Court with Justice John M. Harlan, he went to Harvard, where he has taught since 1961. He was solicitor general of the United States, the advocate for the United States in the Supreme Court during the second Reagan administration, and a justice of the Supreme Judicial Court of Massachusetts from 1995 to 1999. In addition to teaching and writing, he has litigated numerous issues as a private lawyer, including the constitutionality of flag desecration statutes for the American Civil Liberties Union, the proper courtroom use of scientific evidence, and whether the attack on the World Trade Center constituted one occurrence or two. He is the author of eight books on legal and philosophical subjects. In 1959 he married Anne Summerscale, whom he met while they were students in Oxford. They have two children and five grandchildren.